DON'T GIVE IN, GIVE CHOICES

Don't Give In, Give Choices

Winning Your Child's Cooperation

Pat Holt &
Grace Ketterman, M.D.

Harold Shaw Publishers
Wheaton, Illinois

All Scripture quotations, unless otherwise indicated, are taken from the HOLY BIBLE, NEW INTERNATIONAL VERSION®. NIV® Copyright © 1973, 1978, 1984 International Bible Society. Used by permission of Zondervan Publishing House. All rights reserved.

The authors wish to acknowledge their indebtedness to the foundational work of Erik Erikson and Abraham Maslow on the stages of childhood (see *Childhood and Society*, 2nd ed. by Erik Erikson [New York: Norton, 1950, 1963] and on basic human needs (see *Motivation and Personality* by Abraham Maslow [New York: Harper & Row, 1954, 1970]).

ISBN 0-87788-166-9

Edited by Miriam Mindeman and Joan Guest

Cover design by David LaPlaca

Library of Congress Cataloging-in-Publication Data

Holt, Pat, 1943-
    Don't give in, give choices / by Pat Holt and Grace Ketterman.
      p. cm.
    Includes bibliographical references.
    ISBN 0-87788-166-9
    1. Decision-making in children—United States. 2. Child psychology—United States. 3. Discipline of children—United States. 4. Child rearing—United States. I. Ketterman, Grace H. II. Title
    BF723.D4H65   1997
    649'.6—dc21   97-20097
                                                  CIP

03 02 01 00 99 98 97

10 9 8 7 6 5 4 3 2 1

Contents

Acknowledgments

This book is the consequence of the gift of choice we were graciously given by Harold Shaw Publishers, and, most especially, by Editorial Director Joan Guest. Thank you for allowing us the privilege to write.

Joyce Farrell is the angel agent of every author's dreams. Thank you, Joyce, for your continuing gift of encouragement.

Pat's husband, Dave, is the best choice of all. The wonderful consequences continue through the years.

Those who have given prayer as the gift of choice have given the best gift of all. Thank you dear friends: Trudi Ponder, Liz George, Dale & Cindy Hindman, The WVCA Staff, Jeanne Mikusky and MOMS-IN-TOUCH, Bobbi Bourbonnais—"GLO-BO," as well as our dearly beloved parents and our children—Gary, Candice, and Andrew.

Pat Holt

Please note: Though all the examples used here are true, the names and other details have been changed to protect the privacy of all those who shared with us their personal struggles and victories.

Introduction

A good laugh is sunshine in a house.
Thackeray

New parents typically envision a home where laughter is heard often and enjoyed by the entire family. Moms and dads dream of a home free from the problems of their personal backgrounds. In spite of their growing awareness of the size of their responsibility, moms and dads find joy in their new roles as parents. With the thrill of each event—the first sweet gurgle, the first dimply smile, the first kick of wee feet, the first grasp of tiny fists, the first shaky step, the first spoken syllable—parental excitement is renewed.

Then, as the years go by, family life seems to take one of two directions. The parents experience either more enrichment with greater opportunities for shared laughter and enjoyment, or they find parenting becoming a series of growing disappointments. For those families living with disappointment, shared laughter becomes an infrequent visitor.

Don't Give In, Give Choices is designed to empower parents at each stage of their child's development. We bring to this book our personal experience as parents, as well as our professional experiences as medical doctor, child psychiatrist, educator, and school administrator. We know that parents can guide children into patterns of wise decision making, and these are the steps that help:

1. Providing children with limited, age-appropriate choices

2. Requiring children to make their own decisions from the choices provided

3. Letting kids assume responsibility for the consequences of each choice

4. Avoiding rescuing a child from the consequences of a poor choice

5. Being consistent in giving both choices and consequences

6. Maintaining a warm, teaching attitude (not angry or threatening)

These six steps help children make responsible choices and accept responsibility for the choices they make. The steps also guide children to make increasingly better choices as they grow and to trust parents who have proven to be consistent and affirming.

Our vision is an ever-increasing number of homes filled with joyous laughter from hearts that love God and each other.

1

Where the Idea of Choices and Consequences Came From

Destiny is not a matter of chance; it is a matter of choice.
Author Unknown

We have never met a parent who has not struggled with parenting. A parent who does not admit to having difficulties either is totally unaware of the truth or is living in a state of proud and self-deceptive denial.

Children have an uncanny ability to humble parents and other authority figures. Even preschoolers routinely outwit those who are supposedly in charge. When parents and teachers get together, there are always embarrassing stories to share.

Pat knows all too well what it is like to be utterly humiliated as a young and inexperienced teacher. This story of her first day of teaching is adapted from her book, *Ten Myths that Damage a Woman's Confidence*.

> My first day of teaching was disastrous. I went into the classroom fully equipped with a degree, a credential, a creative lesson plan, a big smile, a great outfit, and the self-confidence that others had given me. "You can do it!" they had said. "You are so

good with children!" they had assured me. "The kids will love you!" they had gushed.

In a matter of five minutes, however, the class of eighteen EMR/EH (Educable Mentally Retarded/Emotionally Handicapped) students had destroyed me. They were totally out of control. Within thirty minutes the entire school was well aware that the new teacher was no good. And they were right! If you can't control them, you can't teach them!

I was utterly mortified and did not know what to do. I had signed a contract and was expected to complete the year. What a joke! Getting through that first day seemed like a never-ending nightmare! And at three o'clock I realized that nightmare was my reality!

In despair and confusion, I prayed. I thought God had wanted me to be a teacher, to help and encourage children. Then why was I turning out a complete failure?

From the parental perspective, many of you can relate to this experience. You probably wanted to become a parent. You may have read some books or taken a class to prepare. You thought you were somewhat ready. But the reality of daily life as a parent and the moment-by-moment stress have left you perplexed. Your experience has robbed you of whatever parental self-confidence you may have had. You might be wondering, *Why did I ever think I could be a good parent?* or, *Where is God in all of this?* Pat describes the soul searching she did:

I confess that I was full of anger. No one likes to be humiliated in public. Why did it have to happen on my first day on the job? What could I do about it? I was at a complete loss. Despairing and helpless, I cried out, *I have no idea what to do! All the reading and classes and education have failed me. I must know how to discipline these children.*

The students were already completely out of control. The classroom was like so many homes where there is a power struggle. The kids had the power, and the teacher had the struggle! The more common ways of trying to control children, like spanking, are not options for teachers. The law with good reason prohibits teachers from touching children. And some of the kids were bigger, stronger, and faster than Pat anyway. Further, if she had resorted to screaming, it would only have let the children know how out of control she was. Screaming also would have magnified their responses of anger and rebellion. (Screaming is dealt with in our book, *When You Feel Like Screaming: Help for Frustrated Mothers.*)

What about reasoning with the children and calmly discussing the problem of discipline and cooperation? What was there for them to talk about with the teacher? They'd won. It was their classroom. They were in charge. Pat had already lost the battle of the first day and was well on the way toward retreating in complete defeat. Pat continues:

> After much thought and prayer, the answer came to me. I began to give the children choices as to what they would do and when they would do it. The choices were limited: "Do you want to do this or that? It's your choice." Though I was still terrified, I was amazed to see the plan actually worked. The children loved having the power of making the decision. And, to my relief, the choices advanced both learning and control in the classroom.
>
> When my students didn't want either of the choices given, I was at first at a loss. Then I realized that I must give them in advance not only the limited choice, but also the consequence if neither choice was accepted. For example, a child could choose to do Math or Reading at a certain time, and he or she knew this was the only choice. If the student chose to do neither Math nor Reading, he or she knew that the consequence was losing the op-

portunity to do something special later on. In my particular classroom, we had a kitchen where the children could enjoy cooking, serving, even washing the dishes. If students did not accept either of the choices given, they would lose the privilege of working in the kitchen—something they really enjoyed.

The key was to know what was meaningful to each child and to use that as the positive or negative consequence. Not only did the children know that they could lose opportunities by refusing to make good choices, they also knew that making good choices guaranteed them opportunities to do things they liked to do.

Leaving the decision up to the child had amazing results. The authority figure (in this case, the teacher) could never be accused of being unfair. The students knew exactly what was expected, they had the power to choose, and they knew exactly what would happen if they refused to accept the choices given.

A peace began to settle on the classroom. Truly, this was nothing short of a miracle. Day after day I wondered, *Can this last?* It did. Naturally, the choices changed from time to time as did the consequences. The choices were determined by what students needed to accomplish academically or behaviorally. The consequences were determined by what was important to each child at any given moment.

As time went by, the children and I discussed possible choices and consequences together. The choice to obey or disobey was left up to the child, and the earned consequence (of choosing well or poorly) was the mutual responsibility of the child and me. If the consequence was something positive, it was a delight to give. And if the consequence was something negative, such as the withdrawal of a privilege, it became the responsibility of the child to accept that consequence. After all, the child knew in advance what the choices were and what the consequences would be. It was my job to make certain that the choices and consequences were appropriate and to always be consistent. I could only demonstrate that I was worthy of trust by following through on both positive and negative consequences. The students knew that they would have to assume responsibility for their choices.

Pat maintained a caring attitude throughout. She let the students know she was sorry when they had to miss out on their special privilege because of a poor choice. Yet she held firm. Pat describes the great things that happened in her classroom as time went on:

> To see the leap in maturity of the children that year was astounding. Later in the year, the class actually became a model. There wasn't a week when I didn't have at least two or three observers—college students, supervisors, and teachers from my district or other districts—who came to see this successful special education class. They asked questions and sought help and advice.
>
> Surprisingly enough, my miserable weakness in disciplining and controlling children was becoming a strength. The more I used choices and consequences, the easier it got. I discovered that the gift of choice and consequence worked with all types of children in a huge variety of settings. It worked in homes, schools, and churches. It worked with two-year-olds and teens. I used this plan at home and found it extremely effective with my own children. And I knew that if the principle could work for me, it could work for anyone.

Pat is convinced after more than thirty years of working with parents, children, volunteers, and teaching professionals, and after seeing the idea illustrated so fully in everyday life, that the principle of giving choices and consequences is a priceless parenting jewel available to every mom and dad. We hope that you will discover how this principle can bring joy and peace into your home and at the same time help to build your children's character.

2
Why Parents Give In . . . (Just This Time)

"I want to do what's best for my child!"
A quote from a parent

We have never yet spoken to a parent who made a conscious commitment to give up parental responsibility, to give in, to let the child win and run the household. The parents we talk to know that the parent is to be in charge and to help form the character of the child. Then how does "giving in" happen in homes of bright parents who are devoted to their children and dedicated to doing the right thing?

There are at least six reasons why parents give in ". . . just this time." Each reason is very understandable, can be easily rationalized, and even makes sense at the time of the confrontation. But each is dangerous and develops destructive parent/child patterns that are extremely difficult to change. You may find an explanation for your parenting behavior in one or more of the following:

- **"I don't know what to do!"** These parents are very sincere. They mean well. They want to do what's right. But the vast majority have not had good role models from their own parents. Many times they tell us that their goals are to be different from their parents. Yet, without even realizing it, they slip into emulating the parenting patterns they saw in their childhoods. Overcoming past behavior patterns is a formidable task. It takes the diligence, focus, and concentration of an athlete in training. Learning about choices and consequences is part of that training.

- **"I'm too busy!"** These parents speak the truth. They are overwhelmed with a deluge of *have-tos* that tug at every moment of the day. They find little time for such necessities as thinking through the consequences of giving an ultimatum, formulating future parenting plans, or designing appropriate choices. This is a short-sighted perspective. The quickie decision too often ends up taking a toll on future time that cannot even be calculated. Busy parents don't have time to waste on making mistakes.

- **"I'm too tired!"** We speak to a host of weary parents every week. Their lives are incredibly complicated. These parents are pulled in so many directions and have so much to do that parenting just pulls the plug on their final bit of energy. They are too tired to argue with children who have endless energy when it comes to getting their own way. Children seem to delight in mercilessly badgering such parents until they give in. Believe it or not, though, arguing and debating with a child can be avoided, regardless of how strong-willed the child may be. Giving your spirited child the gift of choice can revive your energy and revitalize your spirit.

- **"Giving in (just this once) works for me!"** These parents are not fooled. They realize they are being manipulated by their children. For them, giving in is no big deal. In the early years of parenting, they find it amusing. They are pleased to have children who are so bright, so clever, and they are certain those children will do well in life. "Nobody will ever get the best of my child!" But the down side of this is that these children grow up believing that their word is law, that the world revolves around them, that they are supreme in the universe, and that no other authority figure deserves to be heard or respected. These children grow up self-centered and rebellious, blaming everyone else when things go wrong. For these parents, learning to give age-appropriate choices and consequences will help channel the child's innate rebellion into acceptance of responsibility.

- **"I just want my child to be happy!"** On a superficial level, this sounds like a reasonable goal. What parent doesn't want a happy child? A happy child is easier to live with than an unhappy child. And in a world of escalating evil and tragedy, happiness seems to be more elusive and therefore more desired. Parents who overemphasize the goal of happiness and give in over and over are shocked to discover that their children are turning into unhappy, raging tyrants. Happiness can never be the goal. Happiness is a by-product of character. In people who are developing a strong character, there is a dramatically higher level of happiness than in those who live to chase after the next good time.

- **"I feel so guilty!"** Parents worry. Most of them experience feelings of guilt about practically everything they are or are not doing for their children. They also feel guilty for screaming, for misjudging situations, for spending too little time with their children, for not having money to do what everyone else does, for being single parents, for having a child with a challenge or disability, for experiencing gut-wrenching inadequacy in parenting. There is so very much to feel guilty about when parenting! But absolutely no one parents perfectly. Dr. Michael Meyerhoff, executive director of The Epicenter Inc., a family advisory and advocacy agency, says,
    If people were intended to be perfect parents, the

Almighty would have endowed everyone with the patience of Job, the wisdom of Solomon, the strength of Samson, and the will of G. Gordon Liddy. Even so, you should note that none of the above was ever required to spend a whole day at home with three kids under the age of 5. I doubt any one of them would have survived that test with his reputation intact.

- **"Progressive parents respect their children's rights."** A growing number of intellectual parents have come to believe in treating children as equals. True, their value is equal to that of adults. But they do not have the wisdom to function as equals with their parents. The healthy parent is the tool with which a child learns wisdom.

Of course, there may be other reasons why parents give in. Whatever the reason, though, we can all see the negative consequences of such a habit. Now let's focus on how giving choices and consequences can reverse these damaging patterns.

3
How Giving
Choices Works

*Everyone, sooner or later, sits down
to his banquet of consequences.*
Robert Louis Stevenson

Parents love to give their children gifts. They often
spend enormous amounts of money to provide a variety
of gifts for their children. Out of hearts of love, parents
sacrifice to provide trips and vacations, educational and
athletic opportunities, and a vast number of "things" to
make their children's lives rich and full and to provide
for their future. Of all the gifts that a parent can give a
child, however, the gift of learning to make good choices
is the most valuable and long-lasting. It can also be
given regardless of the financial condition of the parent.

Choice is a gift that a child will open each time a
decision is needed. Choice is a gift that grows stronger
with use, and it is up to parents to provide the daily
opportunities that will strengthen the gift. It is also the
parent's responsibility to give this gift in the right way,
with wisdom and discretion, with consistent love and
forgiveness, and with optimism about the child's growth
in successful decision making.

As a parent, you will see this gift affect many more
people than your own children. Each time children make
a decision and assume the responsibility for that choice,
their character grows. As they build on bit by bit through

years of increasingly wise decisions, they reach the place
where they are helping to build character and strength
in others wherever God leads them as grown children.

This is especially true in the family. You train your
children through giving them the gift of choice, and that
role modeling will pave the way for them to train their
own children. The character traits of kindness, self-
control, respect, obedience, honesty, and responsibility
can be passed from generation to generation just as
surely as any negative behavior can be passed on to future generations.

Three Kinds of Homes

A very young child is given the opportunity to choose
in a rather small package. To them, this gift takes the
form of "either . . . or." In order to see just how effective
this plan is, let's peek into three homes run in three different ways. The responses of the child and mother give
an insight into different styles of parenting.

The chill of autumn is in the air. Mothers across the
land silently unite to provide their little ones with a
"good, hot breakfast," i.e., oatmeal or some similar con-
coction. A majority of preschoolers also unite in vocal
opposition to this idea.

In the **autocratic** home, the conscientious mother has
verified the weather report, checked outside to confirm it,
and now she has the cereal ready. She proudly announces,
"It's cold out today, so you'll have a hot breakfast."

Three-year-old Jeffrey takes one look at the goo-like
mixture and gives his verdict: "I hate this yucky stuff."

Mom doesn't want an early morning confrontation
that wastes a lot of time, so she tries a reasonable approach. "All the big boys eat hot cereal, and you will
too."

At this point, Jeffrey doesn't care what the so-called
big boys are eating and wants no part of the porridge.
He says defiantly, "I won't eat this yucky stuff."

Mom becomes adamant: "You will eat it, and you will

eat it right now!" The power struggle is off to an early morning start.

In the **permissive** home, Mom is already running late. Since oatmeal is easy and available, it's hastily assembled. She coaxes her disheveled son to the table saying, "Mommy has made something really special for you today."

Three-year-old Steven is not impressed. (He's already heard that story at least a million times.) He looks in the bowl and immediately revolts. "I don't want any of that stuff!"

Mom moves instantly into her cajoling method of operation. "Your friend Ryan eats it."

Steven responds, "I don't care. I won't eat it!" Mom takes a taste. "Mmmm-good. Try just one bite for Mommy." Steven adamantly shakes his head, mouth closed.

"It will make you a big boy like Daddy. Do it for Daddy."

No way.

After a few more futile attempts, Mom unloads her last option. "Mommy will buy you something at the toy store if you eat three bites." At this point, provided that there is something he really wants at the toy store, Steven may eat a bite or two (not three), grimacing the entire time while Mom tells him how wonderful he is.

In the home where the idea of **choices** and consequences is known, understood, and used, the mother knows the weather forecast but, more importantly, she knows her son, Brock. She also knows that almost no human being on earth likes being told exactly what to do, where to go, or what to eat. She knows that Brock responds to choices and likes to feel in control of making decisions. She also knows it's important to give him very simple decisions at his tender age of three. Yes, she would like to have him eat oatmeal or something similar, but she knows that the vitamin and nutritional content of other cereals she purchases is comparable, so she sees the issue as more a matter of taste than a nutritional problem.

This mom gives Brock a choice of two cereals, one that she knows he likes and one, the oatmeal, that she would like him to cultivate a taste for. She says, "This morning we're having cereal. Would you like Corn Whammies or oatmeal?"

The chances are very likely that Brock will select what he already likes. So what? We all like to eat what we like, and not everyone enjoys trying new things, especially in the morning. Why would a three year-old-child be any different? Brock has been given a choice based on relatively similar nutritional value. He has chosen, has felt the independence and power in making a decision. Now he will eat the cereal and be on his way. A power struggle has been avoided. The warmth of love felt by mother and son in this case exceeds the warmth to be gained by oatmeal.

Either . . . Or Choices

The choice given to Brock is typical of good choices for young children:

- We will go either to this restaurant or that one. Which do you prefer?
- We will have either hamburgers or hot dogs. Which do you want?
- Would you rather put away your clothes first or your toys?
- You must help either set the table or dry the dishes. Which would you rather do?

You will notice that in the "either . . . or" choice, there is really no consequence. The choice not selected is simply eliminated. The young child needs to build a foundation of making decisions, just as the parent needs to learn how to give limited, appropriate choices. In the choices mentioned, there is no bad choice, merely two acceptable ones. That is the way it must begin for the mutual success of both parent and child.

When . . . Then Choices

After both parent and child have experienced repeated success with "either . . . or" choice making, it's time to try the more complicated "when . . . then" form of choice. Here are some examples:

- When you have finished picking up your room, then I will help you clean it.
- When you have finished your homework, then you may turn on the TV.
- When you say *please*, then you may leave the table.
- When you bring up your grade to a C (or whatever is realistic), then you may go here or there.
- When you have completed all your chores, then you may take the car.
- When you can pay for the insurance, gas, and car repairs, then you may have a car.

When offering a "when you have . . . then you may . . ." choice, it is wise always to mention the less desirable activity before the more desirable one. Notice that with this more sophisticated "when . . . then" type of choice, a consequence is implied. It becomes obvious that until breakfast is finished, there will be no playing outside. The choice of whether this means five minutes or two hours is entirely up to the child because the parent has said, "When you have finished your breakfast, then you may go outside and play."

It is crucially important to give young decision makers some feedback. Perhaps at bedtime, or after a particularly difficult choice, parents need to help a child see what was good (or not so good) about a decision. It's a good chance to meet each child's basic need for approval and also a means of reinforcing logical thinking.

When offering children choices, the parent does not *make* them do anything. The child chooses. Isn't that what happened in the Garden of Eden?

Grace and Pat are fond of telling this little story:

Years ago, there was a boy named Larry who attended school in a rural one-room school house. The school teacher expected instant obedience. If she didn't get it, she applied the ruler of correction to the knuckles. Larry had been given many hits by the ruler, but still he did not obey as was expected. The teacher warned him that if he kept being defiant, he would be spanked in front of the entire school.

On one particular day, Larry kept getting out of his seat. The teacher warned him repeatedly but still he defied her. Finally, she did as she had said, spanking him hard and long in front of all the students, most of them younger. The school teacher then said in a stern voice, "I trust that you have learned your lesson. Now go back to your seat, and sit down for the rest of the day."

With an angry look on his face, Larry went back to his seat, sat down, and yelled back at her, "I'm sitting down on the outside, but I'm standing up on the inside!"

Too many children today are "sitting down on the outside, but standing up on the inside" because they have not been given the opportunity to choose through the years, and so they are rebelling. The authority figures in their lives have not allowed them the freedom to make decisions that would build their confidence, motivate them, and minimize the power struggle.

Such children have not learned to make the small "either . . . or" choices. They have not experienced the implied consequences of the "when you have . . . then you may" form of choice making. They have never learned to make appropriate choices, so when they rebel, their choices bring disaster to their own lives, to the lives of their parents, and to other lives they touch.

The Benefits of Choice

When a child grows up being allowed to make choices,

essential areas of his or her personal development are being strengthened many times during the day. What are these areas of development?

- *The child learns respect.* A parent shows the child respect by allowing the child to make decisions. Each time a parent gives a child the opportunity to make a choice, that parent is saying, "I love you. I understand that you are made in the image of God and you are worthy of respect. I respect you enough to allow you to make a choice."
- *The child's confidence grows.* Success breeds success. With each wise choice a parent gives, the parent demonstrates love and respect to the child. With each wise choice a child makes (whether to eat a certain cereal, to accomplish a task around the house, or to get and keep employment), the child's confidence grows in his or her ability not only to choose but also to perform in the future.
- *The child is motivated.* Nothing decreases motivation like waking up in the morning knowing that someone else will tell you what to do every moment and that you will have no part in the decision-making process. No parent wants that. No child wants that. On the other hand, nothing increases motivation like knowing that you are the key factor in the decision process, and that the decisions you make will determine not only what you eat and wear, but also what will happen to you during the day. The child who is held responsible for consequences will be highly motivated to make increasingly wiser decisions.
- *Secure parent/child bonds are built.* An atmosphere of no choices is the breeding ground for rebellion. Put yourself in the place of your child. Would you rather be given a choice or be told that you must "do this," "do it my way," and "do it right now"? Besides developing respect, confidence, and motivation in your child, providing appropriate choices also eliminates the parent/child standoff.

Natural Consequences

There are two types of consequences—natural and logical. Natural consequences follow the laws of nature. Charles Stanley once said, "We reap what we sow, more than we sow, later than we sow." If we stop to think about it, we recognize that we depend upon many laws to govern the world. In physics, there is the universal law of gravity. We know it, and we respect it. A person who walks off a tall building is not going to change the law of physics, no matter what he believes about gravity. And if he challenges that law, he'll experience severe consequences.

The idea of consequences—that every choice results in at least one consequence and almost always multiple consequences—can be seen as a law of life, one that operates just as faithfully as the law of gravity. Someone has said, "Sow a thought, reap an action. Sow an action, reap a habit. Sow a habit, reap a lifestyle. Sow a lifestyle, reap a destiny."

We can see that a harvest of consequences comes from our choices and the choices of our children. As parents who love our children, we don't want them to suffer a lifetime of regret and sorrow for the consequences of poor choices. So we must take action. We must teach them to make wise choices from their earliest years, and the only way to do that is to allow our children to assume the responsibility for the consequences of each choice. Accepting responsibility for a consequence trains children to make wiser future choices.

Natural consequences happen as a result of natural causes, usually from something in the environment. Many of life's lessons can be taught most effectively if we let our children experience natural consequences without intervention. A science teacher sent a student into the woods to observe a cocoon. The student watched intently as the butterfly's wings began to break through the silken fibers. Watching and waiting, the student grew impatient. It was taking so long, and the butterfly was putting forth such enormous effort with uncertain results. Unable to stand the seeming futility of the struggle any longer, the student reached out and tenderly helped the butterfly out of the cocoon. Pleased with the result, he watched as the butterfly flew a few feet, then spiraled to the earth and died. Aghast, the student hurried back to the teacher, who then explained, "When you reached in to help, you deprived the butterfly of the opportunity to strengthen its wings in the struggle that was essential for life."

Just as the butterfly had to struggle to gain strength for survival in the outside world, so our children must struggle in order to mature effectively. Rescuing our children, protecting them, and preventing them from experiencing the consequences of their choices will result in their becoming crippled adults who will never "fly" with strength, confidence, and independence.

Even conscientious parents don't always allow their children to experience natural consequences. Out of hearts full of love and service to their children, these parents rescue their children. Parents who rush in to save their children are really saying, "You can't take care of yourself. I can. See—you need me to help you!"

In the following example, notice how two mothers made very different choices about consequences. Also notice the long-range effects of the mothers' choices.

The first time Ben's mother discovered that her first grader had forgotten his lunch, she was frantic. Although she was late for an important appointment and kept others waiting, she raced to school with the all-important lunch. This scenario happened repeatedly for the next two years. The school secretary even heard Ben castigate his mother on occasion: "Where have you been? I'm hungry, and my class has already gone to lunch!" His mother was apologetic and vowed to do better next time!

Of course a "next time" was guaranteed because this mother chose to be a rescuer and to enable her son to continue the irresponsible behavior of forgetting. No doubt this parental training carried over as well into other areas such as forgetting to return library books on time and forgetting to bring papers home to be signed.

Kimberly's mother acted quite differently when her six-year-old daughter forgot her lunch for the third time. This mom understood that this provided an opportunity to develop responsibility in her daughter. Kimberly's mom told her daughter that if she forgot her lunch again she would not make the lunch delivery.

Soon Kimberly forgot her lunch again. And, being a mother who could be trusted by her daughter to follow through on her word, Kimberly's mother did *not* deliver the lunch to school.

The result? Kimberly not only survived, she thrived. The school provided milk and crackers, and willing friends shared. Meanwhile, Kimberly learned a valuable lesson. That afternoon Kimberly told her mother about the makeshift lunch and how she had wanted her own lunch. When her mother asked her what she would do next time, Kimberly responded that she would remember her lunch. "How will you remember it?" her mother asked next, and as they continued to talk, Kimberly came to realize that putting her lunch in her backpack by the door would help her to remember it in the future.

Because of her mother's action, Kimberly learned a new way of remembering her lunch (as well as other things necessary for school). She also learned that her mother considered her worthy of the responsibility of remembering her own lunch. Soon Kimberly's mom will give her more responsibility.

Which of these two children has more confidence? The child who is learning to assume responsibility is growing in capabilities. When a person's capabilities grow, his or her confidence grows also. On the other hand, when children are repeatedly rescued from consequences and responsibility, their emotional development is hampered, and they are left weak, dependent, and vulnerable.

Here are some other common examples of natural consequences:

- It's raining. Your child leaves the house without boots or umbrella. Getting wet is the natural consequence.

- It's a cold day. Your child forgets to take a coat. Getting cold is the natural consequence.

- Your child leaves the house without breakfast. Becoming hungry at school is the natural consequence.

- Your child leaves a wallet containing money on the school playground. Losing the money (and the wallet) is a natural consequence.

Allowing a child to experience results like these is an excellent way to teach responsibility. Nevertheless, there are certain rather obvious times when a wise parent may not permit natural consequences:

- When there is danger to the child. Parents cannot allow natural consequences of actions such as playing in the street, petting an angry dog, or getting close to a swimming pool without knowing how to swim.

- When there is danger to other persons or their property. Parents cannot permit the natural consequences of a child's dropping Grandma's antique vase. A parent also would not allow a child to drop an infant sibling just because the child needed to learn that babies do not bounce!

- When the results of behavior are serious but not immediately apparent. Although parents recognize the importance of oral hygiene, a child may not see the necessity of brushing teeth regularly and carefully. A good parent doesn't risk dental problems by waiting for children to experience the consequences of not brushing.

Logical Consequences

In contrast to natural consequences, logical consequences do not happen automatically. Instead, they are
established by the parent or authority figure and demonstrate to the child what results will logically follow a
particular choice. Logical consequences are related di-
rectly to the choices made. These consequences can be
either positive or negative, depending upon the choice
made. As parents, our goal is to encourage our children
to behave responsibly, and so we must administer these
logical consequences in a firm, loving manner, without
anger or hostility.

There are three questions a parent needs to ask before
specifying a consequence. Asking these three questions
will ensure that the consequence is logical and that it
will not trigger rebellion.

1. Is the consequence related to the behavior?

If your child messes up the kitchen, having the child
clean up the kitchen would be a related and logical consequence, while grounding the child would not be a related or a logical consequence. The child needs to learn
how to clean up messes, and this is the ideal teaching
time.

"But my child doesn't know how to clean up messes!"
you may say. Of course not. Although children are born
to make messes, no child is born with an innate ability
to clean up a mess. Yes, it is faster and easier for Mom
to clean up the mess rather than train the child to clean.
But remember, we are striving to build responsibility. We
also want to teach our children necessary life skills.
Learning how to clean up a mess is a primary skill. The
child must learn that after making a mess, he or she will
always be expected to clean it up.

In the early years, the parent needs to help the child
clean up. At first, this means that the parent will do 110
percent of the cleanup. The little one will make more of
a mess while trying to be "Daddy's best helper." The

child will learn by imitating the parent. Little by little, day by day, the child will learn the skill of cleaning up messes. Both the child and the parent will be justifiably proud as this life skill is developed. The child will have the confidence in his or her ability to learn a very important skill. The parent will be thrilled to have taught something so vital and overjoyed to save the time and energy of having to clean up for the child.

The story of Jonah shows how God relates consequence to behavior. Jonah chose to totally defy the command of the Lord to go to Nineveh. In fact, God allowed Jonah to choose to go by ship in the opposite direction. Then God used that ship, the sailors, the sea, and a whale as a means of bringing to Jonah consequences closely related to his choice to disobey.

2. Is the consequence respectful to the child?

Demeaning your child in front of friends is not treating that child with respect. Screaming at your child in hasty, uncontrolled anger is also not a respectful consequence. In time, your child will scream back, and you will know why. It is demeaning and humiliating to attack a child with such comments as, "Why can't you ever . . . ?" "How many times do I have to tell you?" "I told you so!" and "When will you ever learn?" This will result in angry rebellion or withdrawal in hurt, quiet anger.

Each time you scream disrespectfully at your child, it is as if a poison has been injected that spreads and kills the fragile cells of confidence. Without confidence, your child cannot achieve her or his potential. Instead, that child will become increasingly anxious, insecure, and angry. Because parents aren't perfect, and they aren't always under control, we wrote the book, *When You Feel Like Screaming*. Almost every parent has a problem in this area sometime during the child-rearing years.

If you demonstrate respect for your child in disciplinary situations, your child will learn to respect, trust, and love you, while at the same time learning the life lesson you're trying to teach. A respectful consequence always takes into account the relationship between you and your child. If there are old, long-standing patterns of resentment and power struggles, few consequences or threats will work. Your child may have literally lost the capacity to care. Loss of dessert, TV, playtime, or other privileges may mean little to an angry, hurt child. Such a child will often gain more satisfaction and a stronger sense of power from holding out against you at all costs than he or she could gain by giving in and earning a certain privilege. Parents must consistently communicate love and respect in words and actions.

God showed respect to his defiant, disobedient, but dearly loved human creation. In the Garden of Eden, God gave Adam and Eve a choice and a consequence, in advance. They made their choice, and, of course, God knew exactly what the humans had done. When confronting them, however, God demonstrated respect. Rather than lashing out, God allowed them to give their side of the story. We don't really need to look any further for a role model.

3. Is the consequence reasonable?

It is not reasonable for a child who has not completed homework to write 25, 50, or 100 times, "I will not forget to do my homework." It is reasonable for a parent to expect a child to accept the school's consequence for not doing the homework.

Likewise, grounding a child for a month after two infractions of curfew is also not reasonable, nor is it reasonable to take away a child's bike for two weeks because the helmet was forgotten once.

Sometimes parents think up reasonable consequences and sometimes they don't. Brenda, a single parent with three children, often came home exhausted. When she did, she enjoyed playing the piano for relaxation. One especially difficult evening she craved the soothing effect of her music, but the children were watching TV in the same room. Brenda began playing without saying anything to the children. In order to hear the TV, the children turned up the volume. Then Brenda began playing louder so she could hear the piano. This battle of the decibels continued until Brenda lost her temper and yelled at the kids, "There'll be no TV for the next month!" The children stomped off to their rooms and began a month of silent rebellion at a consequence that was clearly out of proportion to the misdeed. If Brenda had been respectful to her children, she would not have just begun playing without letting them know. She might have told them that after their program ended it would be her turn to use the room. Also, having made the mistake and announced an inappropriate consequence, Brenda could have corrected it. She could have admitted it was a mistake and changed the consequence to "time served"—the number of days already spent without TV. It is usually best to limit imposed consequences to the day of the misdeed in preteenaged children. A good rule of thumb is to *make the consequence the least severe one that will teach the necessary lesson.*

Sometimes our children will understand the consequences and accept them as reasonable. Other times, even though they are aware of the consequences in advance, our children will see those consequences as supremely unreasonable when the time comes to accept them. All we can do is to be sure that our consequences are respectful, reasonable, and related to the behavior. We also need to be sure our children know the consequences beforehand whenever possible. The following illustration shows why this is important.

Fifteen-year-old Michelle wanted to go on a weekend ski trip with some of her friends. She asked her parents, assuring them there would be adequate supervision. It sounded like an extravagant idea to her parents, and they had one question: "How are you going to get the money for the trip?" Michelle had casually mentioned that the weekend would cost almost three hundred dollars.

She responded that from baby-sitting she had approximately one hundred dollars. The trip was three weeks away, but she had to pay in advance. In their discussion, Michelle and her parents determined that no extra two hundred dollars was floating around in the family, but that one of the other families was willing to lend Michelle the money. She was ecstatic, but her parents were far less so, reminding her that Christmas was coming and that it would be difficult to pay back the money and still have anything for gifts and the extras of the holiday season.

Michelle was certain it would all work out. She convinced her parents that she had the earning power through her baby-sitting to take care of the loan and Christmas, too. Then Michelle and her parents agreed that the debt would have to be paid before anything else was purchased.

The ski trip was great fun, but soon it was over. Christmas and the two-hundred-dollar debt loomed on Michelle's horizon. Paying back the money was taking longer than she thought. With Christmas less than three weeks away, she still hadn't paid it off. Michelle became desperate and asked her parents to advance her some money for Christmas. They sat down with her and calmly reviewed her choice to go on the ski trip, her choice to accept the loan, and the agreed-on consequence of paying back the loan before buying anything for Christmas. Michelle told her parents, "I'm trying as hard as I can!"

Her parents congratulated her on her conscientiousness in paying off the debt. Then they suggested she call some of the people who used her as a baby-sitter, and let them know she was available. They also suggested she might consider making gifts of baked goods to help relieve the financial stress. Michelle worked even harder. With extra baby-sitting jobs, she paid the debt, earned a little money for Christmas, and was shopping and baking the week before Christmas. She was proud of herself for paying off the loan and being able to earn a little Christmas money. And her parents gave her the praise she deserved.

Her parents then asked, "What would you do next time?"

Michelle replied, "I've been thinking about that. The trip was fun, but so expensive. If I didn't have to borrow money, I might go, but trying to pay off the loan and get ready for Christmas was just too much. I don't want to go through that again."

Allowing children to assume the responsibility for the logical consequences of limited choices empowers them in two extremely important ways. First, it helps children learn to make *wise* decisions. We can define wisdom as the correct use of knowledge, something that is developed slowly and carefully in children as parents provide appropriate choices and consequences, well-deserved praise for making difficult decisions, and kind, honest feedback about poor choices.

The second important effect of allowing children to assume responsibility for consequences is that it helps them develop *strength of character*. As parents allow their children to endure the temporary discomfort of painful consequences, without rescuing them, the children develop inner strength. Character is molded, chiseled, sanded, and refined.

This invaluable combination of wisdom and strength will serve your children well in later years as they face the difficulties and heartaches of life. Wisdom and strength will enable them to emerge not disillusioned or destroyed, but tested and tried.

In the next chapter we will survey the stages of childhood and consider more specific uses of choice.

4
Choices for Infants and Toddlers

Choices are the hinges of destiny.
Edwin Markham

The administrator of a psychiatric hospital once stated, "Good mental health is the ability to make smart decisions." How true, and when you think about it, how obvious.

For parents, the decision making begins before the birth of the child. The expectant parents decide which child-rearing books to read, which tapes or videos to purchase, which classes to attend. They decide whether to take an educational approach to parenting by putting into practice ideas they have come across, or to take an intuitive approach by responding to situations as they come based on innate knowledge and judgment. If you're reading this book, you are probably taking an educational approach, either because that is your nature or because your intuition has let you down. Informed intuition is what is needed.

In applying choices to infants and toddlers, you will note that the parents in our examples do most of the choosing. They choose the way in which they will respond to their children. Later on, the children begin to make clearer choices.

Basic Needs of Children—Birth to Two

The infant and toddler bring to their world basic needs which, if fulfilled, allow them to develop a deep sense of trust. These basic needs include:

- Food
- Warmth
- Shelter
- Boundaries
- Unconditional love
- Approval
- Security
  This last item on the list, security, grows from the consistent, wise, age-appropriate care of loving parents.

After the birth of a child, parental reactions to even the child's cry can monumentally influence the infant. A parent can respond to the crying child with calmness, comfort, and protection, teaching trust and providing security. Or, the parent can react in frustration and anger (even abuse), causing anxiety and fear for the infant. Or, the parent can ignore the infant, leaving the child's needs unsatisfied and creating a climate which offers no security.

Brian's Lament
Three-week-old Brian awakens at two o'clock in the morning. His stomach is empty, and his hunger pains tell him so. Furthermore, his diaper is soggy, and he feels chilly. His parents are sound asleep. Brian "chooses" to cry because his cry is the only means by which he can say, *Help! I'm miserable!* While three-week-old Brian is not actively thinking, *I'm going to scream so Mom or Dad will take care of me*, he is reacting to a situation. It is Brian's parents who must choose and use their thinking ability to teach him.

Babies learn to cry less and trust more when parents are consistent, gentle, and strong. If Brian's parents respond to him lovingly, restoring his comfort and refusing to encourage his nocturnal playfulness, he will learn to go back to sleep, and gradually, to sleep through the night.

It is the way that parents handle the crying that teaches Brian what to do next time. If his parents are slow to respond, but do so when his cries become more insistent, Brian will learn that loud, unceasing noise gets results. He will learn to "hang in there," keep up his demands, and finally get the payoff. If Brian's parents are consistent in the way they respond to his cries and in the length of time it takes them to reach him, Brian will know what to expect. This early training for both parent and child will pay big dividends later on.

Basic Needs of Children—Two to Three Years

Children of later toddlerhood have needs that relate to their desire for independence and exploration. They include:

- Power
- Freedom
- Independence
- Pride and approval for doing well
- Boundaries
- Security

During the critical *tender twos*, a toddler moves from almost total care by parents to a great amount of self care. Toddlers feed themselves, begin to use the toilet, play alone, give up bottle or breast feeding (if they haven't already), and often must learn to deal with older or younger siblings.

This adds up to massive changes for a very small person! The two-year-old wants to be independent, but is reluctant to give up the moment-by-moment physical closeness and assurance the parent has provided. Satisfying the toddler's need for growing freedom within clearly defined boundaries is the parental challenge here, especially because there is an ongoing fluctuation in the balance between these two entities.

You cannot overestimate the importance of loving, consistent discipline at this stage of your child's life. Truly, you, the parents, are sowing seeds. If you sow into the wind at this stage, you will reap the whirlwind of defiance and rebellion. If you sow with love, wisdom, and consistency, as God enables, you will reap the beautiful harvest of a child who has developed strong character. That child will also give you the love and respect you have earned.

Melanie's looks

Melanie's big brown eyes flashed angrily. This two-year-old wanted the brightly printed music books in her mother's rack. The pictures were pretty, and her past experience with old magazines told her that the sound of tearing paper was fun. Even at two years of age she felt very much in charge of life when she ripped up the newspaper.

But here was Mother offering her a box of old magazines and emphatically saying, "Melanie! You may have these magazines or you may come in the kitchen with me." She was even blocking Melanie's access to those other lovely pages. Perhaps if Melanie just waited a bit, her mom would go away. Mom, however, didn't leave. She stayed right there, and her voice said, "I mean business! It's time you learn to stay within your limits. You may NOT play with my expensive sheet music!"

Now both parent and child have choices to make. And it is the actions chosen by the mother which determine what Melanie will learn. Melanie's mom has three options:

- She can indulge her child, let Melanie destroy the music, and replace it.

- She can put the music out of reach, postponing the task of teaching Melanie to live within limits.

- She can use this opportunity, with love that is firm and consistent, to teach Melanie to respect other people's property.

Melanie's mom wisely chooses to teach her child to respect property in these ways:

- Firmly and seriously (but not angrily) restraining Melanie every time she reaches for the forbidden item, saying (and meaning) no, and suggesting an alternative.

- Staying with this struggle until Melanie learns to keep her hands off the music. This might take hours, depending upon the strength of Melanie's will and whether her parents have given in during past confrontations.

- Testing the genuineness of Melanie's mastery of this vital lesson. Melanie's mom might step out of Melanie's range of vision and wait to see if the child touches the music. If she does not, the lesson has been learned for this day.

- Repeating the teaching experience as many times as necessary for Melanie to give up her efforts to grab the music and tear it.

Danny's Nap Time
Two-and-a-half-year-old Danny, trying desperately to look alert, is getting very sleepy. It is past nap time. He is playing with his brightly colored building blocks. His wise mother decides to give him the benefit of choice and consequences. She sets the kitchen timer and reminds him, "Danny, it's nap time. I'm setting the timer. If you want a story, you must have your blocks picked up when the timer rings. If you do not pick up your blocks by the time it rings, you will not have a story before your nap."

Danny, a bright and independent boy, has a choice to make. He can refuse to pick up and throw a fit, or he can pick up and enjoy the promised story. There's a third possibility, too. Danny can see if Mom really means what she says, or if she will forget and read him a story even if he does not pick up the blocks on time.

When children are this age, it is vital for moms and dads to be consistent. Children almost never like to stop playing to do something less fun. When parents fail to follow through, the child becomes confused. It is as if the child wonders, *What's happening? My parents say one thing, but they do something else. They don't mean what they say. Maybe I should run the house.*

Danny's mom understands this concept. She says, "Danny, I saw by your face that you wanted to keep on playing, but I also saw you start to pick up your blocks. I'm proud of you for that! As soon as you're done, let's cuddle in the rocking chair while I read."

Several good things result from this situation. First, this child has observed that his mom can be trusted. She says what she means, and she means what she says the first time she says it. Second, Danny's obedience, even when he didn't feel like it, has been noticed, understood, and rewarded. Third, Danny has realized that his mom loves him, understands him, wants him to obey, and will reward his choice of obedience.

Gail's Temptations

Occasionally parents will attempt to avoid giving a choice or consequence in their parenting. "Let's not talk about it," or "I don't want to even think about it," are comments heard when pressure is being exerted for a decision. What they're really hoping is, *If I don't think about it, it will go away.* But failure to make a choice is a choice. It is a choice to abdicate responsibility, allowing the relentless drift of events to shape the lives of parents and children, rather than assuming the authority parents are supposed to exercise. Some parents abdicate their parental responsibility so persistently that it develops into a habit leading to a crippling inability to make decisions.

Gail was an adorable baby, growing up in a loving home. When she was a toddler, she began to reach out and grab for things. Gail's well-meaning parents didn't want to thwart her curiosity and didn't understand the importance of setting limits. They used the technique of distraction to stop Gail. When Gail reached for a breakable object, they would say, "Look over here, Gail. You like trucks. Let's play with this big truck." This worked for a time but, unfortunately, the technique became less and less effective the more it was used.

When Gail was two and liked to grab things in the grocery store, her parents would say, "Look over here, Gail. You like this. Let's get one of these." By that time, however, the distraction technique was nearly useless. Gail would glance in their direction and then grab what she really wanted with great intensity. She knew what she wanted, and she would not be distracted.

Eventually, since passive control was not working, Gail's parents began to be assertive. Still, they didn't know how to give choices and consequences. They would say, "Don't touch that, Gail . . ." "Gail, get your hands off of that . . ." "Gail, I'm counting. One, two, three . . . when I get to ten you're getting slapped. Eight and a half, eight and three-quarters, nine . . . Gail, I mean it! Get your hands off!" By the time her parents got to nine and seven-eighths, Gail had lost interest in whatever she was touching and was ready to move on anyway.

The parents realized their discipline wasn't working, but they didn't know what to do. "I guess Gail's just a strong-willed child," they would say to friends. Poor Gail. She was given distractions and warnings, countings and slaps—but no choices. Such a pattern in a home will only cause a child's limit testing to grow.

What could Gail's parents have done? Everywhere a two-year-old goes, there are brightly colored things to touch. The grocery store is a treasure chest of such things. Because of this, Gail's parents needed to prepare their child ahead of time for what she would see and what behavior they desired from her. They could have said, "Gail, we are going to the grocery store. You are going to see many things. You may look at them with your eyes, but not your hands. You may not touch anything. IF you obey and do not touch the things in the store, when we get to the cereal section, you may choose your favorite cereal. You may touch the cereal box and hold it. If you touch anything else, you will not be able to pick your favorite cereal."

That's the way to give someone such as Gail choices and consequences. The rest would be up to her. She would have control over her destiny in the grocery store. If she chose to obey, there would be a good reward. If she chose to disobey, she would lose out on the special reward. In this situation, the parents' object must be to be worthy of trust. The child's need is to know that her parents say what they mean and mean what they say. This extends also to the child's response to any negative consequences. If she throws a fit, she needs to know that she will be removed from the scene at once. Of course, such an action is not convenient for anyone, but a wait in the car with a parent until she gains control is one more way to teach a child that Mom and Dad mean business.

Parents of two-year-olds often say, "I can't wait until this stage is over!" Every parent can smile and relate to that. There is one huge problem with this wish, however. If the child-rearing problems, frustrations, and parental inadequacies you are experiencing at this state of development are not dealt with, they will not go away just because the child turns three. They will merely change and surface in other problems that are even more difficult and frustrating. In the twos are growing the seeds of the teens!

This warning is not meant to discourage you, but to encourage you to take action. Results of loving, consistent, wise, age-appropriate discipline come faster than you might think. Actually, parents who are developing strong character in their children will begin to reap results even with a two-year-old.

Gary's Breakfast

Gary was just finishing breakfast. The rule in his house was that he must say *please* after each meal to be taken out of the highchair. Gary and his mom had chatted during breakfast, and they had read a story together. At this point, Gary's mother asked, "Are you ready to get down?" Gary nodded his head. "Say *please*, and you may get down," she added. Gary did not respond. His mother asked again, "Are you ready to say *please*?" Gary shook his head. "Then you are not ready to get out of your highchair," his mother concluded.

She began to do the morning dishes and clean up the kitchen. After several minutes, she reminded Gary, "I will get you out as soon as you ask me politely." She did not belabor the point nor scold Gary for not saying *please* yet. It was his choice to make.

After several more minutes, though, Mom was beginning to get irritated. In her heart, she wanted to let him down. His diaper needed changing—badly—and she wanted to get on with the rest of the day. But also in her heart she realized that this simple act of defiance was a power struggle and, if not handled properly, would be the first of many more. She made a decision to stick it out, and Gary was given the opportunity to make a good choice. She took Gary out to change his diaper and then put him back in his chair.

"Gary," this mother said in an even voice when she was finished in the kitchen, "don't forget that you can get out and go play as soon as you say *please*. Do you understand?" Gary nodded. Then Mom left the kitchen.

What have I started? she asked herself. *What if he doesn't say* please *for the rest of the day? I can see the headlines now—"UNFIT MOTHER LEAVES CHILD IN HIGH-CHAIR FOR TWENTY-FOUR HOURS!"* She shivered. *Please let Gary say* please!

Then she smiled at the ridiculousness of the situation. This was something nobody ever told her about parenting. Feeling somewhat guilty and rather ineffective, she decided to remain firm and see this situation through. She went on with her work as usual, letting Gary sit in the kitchen by himself in the highchair. Every fifteen minutes or so, she checked on Gary and said, "As soon as you say *please* you may get down and play. Are you ready to play?" Once Gary nodded. "Are you ready to say, 'Please get me down'?" Gary shook his head. His mother sighed deeply. *He's as stubborn as I am*, she thought, as she left the kitchen again.

This went on for another half an hour, while his mother was thinking, *What am I going to do with this child? If he's like this now, what does the future hold?*

At long last, Gary's mother asked again, "Do you want to play, Gary?" He gave a vigorous "Yes!" "Do you know what to say?" He nodded. "As soon as you say it, you may get down."

A long moment of silence passed. Then a weak "P-please" was heard. His mother was elated!

"Now you may get down and play!" Gary was helped down and he toddled off to play. His mother sat down, sighed with relief, and wondered what the next meal would bring.

That mother was Pat, and I'm pleased to tell you that incident was the first and last of its kind with my son. He found out early that I said what I meant, I meant what I said, and I could be trusted to follow through.

What if the mom had become impatient with the lack of response and had given in to her son, saying, "Well, I'm going to let you get down this time, but I hope you've learned your lesson and won't ever do this again!" You can be certain that her son would have learned a different sort of lesson. He would have learned that the one who holds out is the winner.

Of course, we know that being consistent and following through is not easy. Pat still vividly recalls how ineffectual she felt during power struggles like this one:

Even though I'd taught for years and knew that giving the gift of choice and consequence was the correct way to discipline, it was still very difficult to follow through in this situation. I really had to pray my way through it, asking God to help me do the right thing and to give my son a heart to obey!

5
Giving Choices to Preschoolers

I took a piece of living clay
And gently formed it day by day . . .
Anonymous

Research in the field of child development indicates that fifty percent of a child's attitudes and habits are established by the time the child is four years old, and that eighty percent of the child's values and attitudes are established by the time the child is eight. Parents do not have much time. Every moment of the early years is crucial. That is why people who are wise in child rearing focus on the early years. Truly, those are the years when the seeds are being sown.

Taking the time and effort to give your children choices and consequences will likely bring you a future harvest of children who know and do what's right. And in order to do what is right for preschoolers, you will need to know something about their basic needs.

Some Basic Needs of Three- to Five-Year-Olds

The child from three to five is exploring the world and learning all sorts of new information about the world and the people in it.

- Time to create and imagine
- Freedom to experience and explore
- Power to choose
- Limits to protect and direct
- Opportunities for fun and learning
- Security

Most threes and fours are able to communicate well. They have good vocabularies, can listen intently for short periods of time, and enjoy discussing ideas with others. While twos are primarily focused on deciding whether to obey their parents or to rebel, threes and fours have added another element to the decision-making process: they are determining how to treat peers and what to do in play activities.

Preschoolers love to create and imagine. They are able to fantasize in ways that involve a great deal of rather complex thinking. They are very busy with their play. For most preschoolers, if parents fail to set limits, they will never take a nap and will collapse from exhaustion . . . right alongside an extremely fatigued parent! It's noteworthy that some preschoolers do not need naps if they go to bed at a reasonable time, but a quiet rest time serves them well and gives parents a break.

Four-year-olds are full of questions. The *whys*, *hows*, and *how comes* are matched only by the *wheres* and *whos*. Fours are curious and will keep on asking. Fours not only gain facts, but they also experience the first glimpse of life in the adult world of knowledge.

Within limits, a preschooler can decide what to wear, which crayons to use, what books to love, and even which playmates to choose. A preschooler won't always choose to take turns, to be obedient, or to follow the rules. The preschooler's need for power and freedom must be balanced with the need for loving, consistent, wise, age-appropriate discipline. In chapter three we looked at some examples of choices that related to preschoolers. Here are some other examples that might be helpful.

Andy's Dawdling

Andy was a four-year-old, freckle-faced bundle of charm. He was extremely well coordinated and learned quickly how to use a ball or a bicycle. But he was very slow when it came to getting dressed and leaving the house. Dressing was an ongoing point of contention between Andy and his mother, especially since she had recently taken a part-time job and had to get Andy to preschool and herself to work on time. Andy was particularly negligent with his shoes. They might be anywhere when it was time to put them on, anywhere except where he looked, of course.

This dawdling is absolutely maddening! Andy's mother thought to herself. *There must be something I can do to make it stop.*

On one particular morning, Andy's mom was nearly ready to leave. Andy had dressed (except for his shoes), finished breakfast, and started playing. One look at his feet was enough to bring steam out of his mother's ears. *Control,* she thought angrily. *I must keep control and not say anything I will regret. What to do . . . ?*

She barely stopped herself from screaming, "I've told you a million times to get on your shoes before you start playing. You have two minutes to find your shoes, and if they aren't on in two minutes, you're going to school without them!" Then she pictured the inevitable in her mind's eye. The two minutes would be up and still the shoes would not be found. She would have to force a screaming, kicking, angry son into the car. The sobbing would continue all the way to school, accompanied by her screams about how many times she had told him, etc., etc. Arriving at school, Andy would have to be forced out of the car, still hysterical and unable to function. The entire school would hear the screeching and see the boy without shoes, and every parent and teacher would be talking about "that woman who let her son come to school without shoes!"

Andy's mother shook her head, still wondering what

to do. She looked at her watch in dismay. Time had not stood still during her fantasy side trip. She had to get out of the house.

Then an idea came. Andy loved his tennis shoes. They were new, and he was certain he could run faster than ever with them. He called them his "racing shoes." But he was not too fond of his slip-on dress shoes, the ones kept in a box on the top shelf of his closet. (Surprisingly enough, both Andy and his mom knew where that pair was!) *That's it!* Mom thought suddenly. *If Andy can't find his tennis shoes, he must wear his dress shoes! That's a logical consequence that is related, responsible, and respectful.*

"Andy," she called in a firm tone. "We are leaving the house in two minutes. You need to find your shoes and put them on either in the house or in the car. If you cannot find your racing shoes, then you may wear your good shoes."

"But I don't like my good shoes. They are slow. I like my racing shoes," Andy responded.

"Then you had better find them now," his mother replied.

Andy rushed here and there searching. Within the two-minute time frame he had found one shoe in the garage, but he could not find the other. And Andy's mom stuck to her decision. "You are responsible for your racing shoes," she stated. "If you want to wear them to school so that you can run fast, then you will need to keep them in a place where you can find them. If you can't find them, then you will need to wear your good shoes. Do you understand?"

Andy nodded. But he wasn't too happy about wearing "slow" shoes all day. Fortunately, there were no important races that day at preschool. And after arriving home, he and his mother formed a search party to find the other shoe, which they did—inside a robot.

"Where do you think you should keep your shoes so you can find them in the morning?" Andy's mother asked.

Andy thought, then answered, "By my bed. Or, maybe in the closet."

"Good thinking, Andy," his mother agreed with a big smile. And from then on, there were very few mornings that Andy did not have his racing shoes on when it was time to leave. Just the idea of having to wear his "slow" shoes kept his "fast, racing shoes" readily available.

The victory in this story was the self-control of Andy's mom. Faced with ongoing frustration with Andy, combined with time pressure, she controlled herself in an extraordinary manner. She demonstrated how a parent who takes the time to think through consequences *before lashing out* will save much bitterness and grief.

Bedtime Battles

Bedtime for preschoolers can be a nightmare for parents who get drawn into a child's game. The Bedtime Game is a favorite for children. Although the variations are endless, there's "one more kiss," "one more story," "one more drink," "one more game," "one more stuffed animal." Once a preschooler gets the hang of the game and develops skill in playing, he or she will want to play the game longer and will have a stronger determination to win. Being the winner in this game means staying up longer, no matter how contrived the excuse may be. "There are four ghosts, two dragons, and three goblins in my room," does not even begin to stretch the imagination of a preschooler!

At first, some parents are amused by the inventiveness of their bright children. The parents will smile, cajole, and bribe. The preschooler knows they are not serious, and so the game continues until the parents wear out. The preschooler never tires of the game! (One of the bigger mistakes parents make is grinning while they correct a child. Parents must keep the desired outcome firmly in mind to maintain a no-nonsense attitude.)

So, what is a parent to do, especially if playing games has become a habit? Parents need to establish themselves as the authority figures in the home. They need to set bedtime limits and make sure they are met. The parents need to say what they mean and mean what they say *the very first time,* instead of waiting until they are tired or disgusted or frustrated, or all of the above.

To do this, a kitchen timer (or similar device) will help. Parents need to decide exactly what the bedtime routine in their home consists of. This might include cleaning up toys, bathing, brushing teeth, and having a story and prayers. The parents have to determine how long this should take in their home. Once this time frame is established so the timer can be set, the child needs to know that the ticking timer tells how long it is until bedtime. The child also needs to know that when the timer rings, there will be no more story, drinks, songs, games, or anything else! The timer will help the manipulated parent to start all over again to establish boundaries of behavior. Then, once the boundaries have been set, it is up to the parent to be consistent, or the standards don't mean a thing.

In this plan to end the bedtime game, the children also need to know what will happen if they do not adhere to bedtime. In advance, parents must establish consequences that will mean something to their children and let the children know what will happen. For example, if storytime is the most important part of the routine to the children, then loss of storytime is the consequence of not respecting bedtime.

The children also need to be encouraged. For example, if your son for three nights is able to control his urge to play instead of getting ready for bed, the parents might reward him by reading an extra story or playing an extra game during the evening before bed. This approach has transformed ugly bedtime nightmares into pleasant bedtime dreams in countless homes!

Leave-Taking Tantrums

The area of preschool and daycare can be fertile ground for parental dilemmas. For some, preschool attendance is a luxurious option. For others, daycare may be a necessity. Whatever the situation, parents must face the problems that saying good-bye can bring. Many parents dread the daily nightmare of trying to get out the door of the daycare. What makes saying good-bye so difficult? Why are there so many problems?

1. *The parent feels guilty.* If the parent, mom or dad, feels guilty about leaving the child, there will be trouble. The child will sense this and react. After a seemingly great start for the first few days in school, the child might begin to get teary and cling. The guilt-ridden parent will often blame the teachers and the school because they encourage the parent to "just leave." But often parents can't "just leave" because they are not ready to leave their children with a substitute parent. The result is an unhappy child, a confused parent, and an aggravated teaching staff.

If you, as a parent, do not feel ready to trust your child to another's care, take a careful look at your income and lifestyle to see if you could avoid childcare for a while. Then consider taking the child to a play group where Mom or Dad is allowed to stay. This, or part-time work, can provide an easy transition into daycare.

We would also like to encourage those of you who have to work. Your children can be helped to understand why that fact is true. Each child can be trained to fit into the family schedule and help out with family duties.

2. *The child attempts to the make the parents feel guilty.* Many moms like to provide a morning or two a week of preschool enrichment for their child to give themselves time off or to spend the time with an infant. All goes well at first. Then that fateful morning comes when the preschooler decides she does not want Mom to leave and lets Mom know by clinging to her or by crying.

The conscientious Mom is stunned! *What has happened? What's going on at this school? My child loved school the first week.* Certainly it is possible that something is wrong. Perhaps there is a problem with a teacher or another preschooler. The parent should check things out to be sure there is no legitimate reason for the change in attitude. If there is no problem, then the parent can be certain that the child is trying to take charge and make her own decision about going to school or not.

This is where the parent has the opportunity to begin to teach, through choices and consequences, the tough character quality of responsibility. The child has a safe, fun place to go and play and learn with other children. That is what the child *will do* for the prescribed period of time. If the parent is firm and loving, and cannot be manipulated, this very common phase will pass. However, if the parent begins to feel anxious, insecure, or guilty, the symptoms will escalate, and this phase will lengthen enormously!

3. *The child fears a new baby will usurp his or her place with Mom.* Most children experience a sense of rejection when seeing a new baby getting a great deal of attention. This may result in a refusal to leave Mom to go to preschool. Mom can help alleviate this insecurity by explaining that she loves the older child as much as the baby. In fact, her love has gone on much longer with the older child. A bit of extra cuddling and attention along with the passing of time will reassure the fears and make the adjustment become a smoother one.

4. *The child experiences separation anxiety.* A child who is well attached to his parents, is sensitive or shy, will often feel anxious when separated from them. The parents can help him adjust by explaining why he needs to be left, how long they will be away, and when they will return. As the child learns that he can trust his parents always to return when they are due, then his anxiety at separation will gradually disappear. But if parents are unreliable about picking up the child on time, his anxiety at separation will continue.

If one has chosen a daycare, preschool, or play group wisely, one does not need to worry about the child. Be confident that your child can thrive away from home if that child knows that you love and care for him or her and can be trusted to come back to pick the child up.

6
Letting School-Aged Children Choose

[I] molded with God's power and art
A young child's soft and yielding heart.
Anonymous

The ages of five to twelve are vital decision-making years. At around seven or eight, children form their own concept of the world in which they live, and this concept stays with them for life. We've already mentioned the research findings that eighty percent of a child's values and attitudes are established by the age of eight. This beautiful poem captures the impressionableness of those early years:

I took a piece of plastic clay
And idly fashioned it one day
And as my fingers pressed it still
It moved and yielded at my will.

I came again when days were past,
The bit of clay was hard at last.
The form I gave it, it still bore
And I could change that form no more.

I took a piece of living clay
And gently formed it day by day
And molded with God's power and art
A young child's soft and yielding heart.

I came again when years were gone.
A man now I looked upon.
And he that early impress wore
And I could change him never more.

Anonymous

This poem poignantly expresses the crucial opportunity and responsibility of parenthood during the formative years.

Needs of Elementary School Children

School-aged children are refining their skills in many areas and learning to relate to others. Their needs include:

- Boundaries that are slowly expanding
- Competence in at least one area
- Opportunities to develop academic and motor skills
- Increasing ability to relate socially
- A beginning understanding of values
- An increasing ability to take responsibility

Homework: The Dreaded Assignment

Although the foundation of responsible character can be laid even before grade school, responsibility is still the foremost lesson for children ages five through twelve. For many families, homework is a major battleground where responsibility is taught or fought.

In the private elementary school where Pat is administrator, the character qualities of kindness, obedience, honesty, respect, responsibility, and self-control are emphasized each day, all through the day. Christlike character is of paramount importance and is emphasized in all areas of curriculum and activities. Nevertheless, every year the same thing happens at each grade level regarding homework. In spite of the fact that the parents have agreed that it is the child's responsibility to get the homework assignment, complete it, and bring it back on time, there are always parents who want to excuse their child when a consequence is given for not completing homework. "It was my fault!" a mom will lament. "I forgot to remind him to put it in his backpack." Another mom will explain, "I found it lying under the mat in the back seat." A dad will excuse his daughter with "She was tired last night." And still another parent will apologize, "They were at their grandmother's house over the weekend."

These parents earnestly want success for their children, but they are somewhat confused. Just because their child makes a mistake about a homework assignment, these parents do not descend on the parent quality scale. Every kid forgets something at some time. So what! Let the child experience the consequence. That will trigger a better memory in the future . . . but only if Mom or Dad doesn't try to excuse, defend, or rescue the child from the consequence.

Forgetting homework is a small thing, but it is an example of an area where parents need to relax, let the child make a mistake, and then let him or her accept the consequence. At stake is the opportunity to build responsibility. The homework problem is just one small step along the path to mature adult responsibility.

If a parent does not get upset over the forgotten assignment, the child will learn that making mistakes is an ordinary part of life. There are consequences to pay, but such a mistake does not mean that a child is bad or incompetent—the message the child receives when Mom or Dad flies off the handle over the child's forgetfulness.

Whose Project Is It?

Elementary school projects! In some parents these three words cause a rush of adrenaline that acts faster than any pill on the market. Implied in these three words are such generally accurate perceptions as "It's for Open House," "They'll be judged," and "They'll be on display for *everyone* to see." Parents pass this fear of comparison along to their children.

Schools must accept their fair share of blame. Many can be justifiably criticized for making Open House a competitive show. In fact, many schools have done away with such competitions in favor of a display of student work that has been done in class. But those schools that put a premium on academic rank still hold competitive events around school projects. In such settings, insecure parents give an enormous boost to making each Open House the "show of shows!"

In this absurd emotional milieu, regardless of what schools may or may not do, parents have choices and consequences. Parents of children with school projects have the choice to play the competitive game or not. So do parents of children in competitive sports like Little League. Parents must carefully evaluate their choices and the consequences in such situations and make the decision as a family. Find out what the child is thinking and what the child does or does not want to do. If the child does not choose to invest a great quantity of time and effort in the project, then the parents would be wise to let the consequence of that choice be reflected in how much time, money, and effort the parents spend on the project.

Wise parents will see the consequences of doing too much work for their child. Too often, the child abdicates responsibility for the project, so the parent leaps in and does more than half the work, complaining about the school and the assignment the entire time. When this happens, the parent has made the choice to do the assignment rather than let the child choose. In effect, then, the parent is complaining about the consequences of a parental choice.

Parents can also use school projects as an object lesson. There is the significant potential for human error in grading and judging large projects. The grade is a subjective assessment by the teacher. If a teacher does not like a particular "style" of doing a project, a poor grade may be given. Children must learn that life is not fair, that well-meaning people make mistakes, and that losing is painful, whether the loss involves a ribbon, a grade, a trophy, a place on the team, or anything else. They can also learn how to be assertive regarding grades by asking for clarification if a grade is not understood.

Many difficulties accompany the building of character qualities like kindness, obedience, honesty, respect, responsibility, and self-control. It takes those tough times of life to make such qualities a reality in the lives of both parents and children.

What about Forgetfulness?

The problem of a child's forgetting is as common as dust in a house. Whether it is forgetting homework or lunches, every parent has at least one story to share. For a view of how two moms handled the same situation in contrasting ways, please refer to chapter 3.

Clearly, forgetfulness is best handled by allowing the child to face the natural consequences of forgetting. However, there is also a time to teach kindness if special circumstances come to play. There are many children who are, indeed, very responsible. They write down their assignments, study for tests in advance, and pack their backpacks before they go to bed. But inevitably that child will also forget something—perhaps her glasses on the day of the field trip to the planetarium, or the batteries that power his science project. In such cases and with children who are not frequent forgetters, a parent may "rescue" the child because the consequences of forgetting are great and because unusual circumstances (dressing differently for the field trip; carrying extra boxes with the science project) may have contributed to the forgetfulness. At such times, the parent is teaching about love, forgiveness, and grace—lessons that are as important to learn as responsibility.

Lisa's Peer Pressure

Elementary-aged children are not too young to face the
problem of peer pressure. Even a nine-year-old can experience pressure to do wrong instead of right. In Lisa's
neighborhood, there were no children her age, so she
spent time with two older girls, ages thirteen and fourteen. One Saturday morning, the other girls invited Lisa
to go to the mall with them. Since they had no way to
get there, they asked if Lisa's mom would drive and she
agreed.

Each girl came to the car with a large shopping bag,
saying they had birthday presents to exchange. When
they arrived at the mall, Lisa's mom arranged to pick
up the girls after they had lunch and exchanged the gifts.

The older girls wanted to eat as soon as they arrived,
but they had no money. When they asked Lisa how
much she had, she told them, and they used her money
to feed all three of them. At lunch, Lisa asked what gifts
the girls were exchanging, and what they were going to
get. They gave vague answers, so Lisa dropped the sub-
ject. After all, it seemed reasonable that the big girls
wouldn't tell her everything. She was just proud to be
in their company.

After lunch, it was time to "shop 'til you drop." Lisa
loved to go to the mall, look at all the beautiful things,
and imagine what she would buy if she could. Since the
girls had taken all her money, she had none to spend.
But that was okay. Today she would look. After all, it
was fun to be with teenagers. And this was the very first
time they had invited her to the mall.

The girls went into several different stores, looking at
things, but not exchanging the birthday gifts. In fact,
when Lisa peeked into one of the bags, she didn't see
much. *Oh well,* she thought. *Maybe they just brought a
really big bag for a small gift, hoping to get something bigger
and better.*

Later on Lisa looked again. There were a lot of things
in both bags now, and none of them were in store bags.

"What are you doing?" she asked the girls.

"Shut up, Lisa. What do you think we're doing? We're shopping!" the girls said sarcastically.

"But you don't have any money!" Lisa retorted.

"Oh really? So what. We've learned to shop without money, stupid!" one of the girls snarled.

"And now, cuz you're such a *nice* little girl, we'll teach you," the other girl taunted.

"Th-that's okay," Lisa whispered. "You don't have to. I don't mind not getting anything."

"But we want you to have something," one of the girls said. "See that jewelry over there?"

Lisa barely nodded.

"Take this bag, go over to where the earrings and bracelets are, and just slide something into the bag."

"But I really don't w-want to," Lisa stammered.

"Do you want to be our friend?" one of the girls asked vehemently.

"Yes," Lisa nodded.

"Then do what I say, or we can't be friends with you!"

The other girl chimed in, "That's right! Take the bag and get a piece of jewelry in it, or we'll never speak to you again!"

Lisa was scared. She knew that stealing was wrong, but she really liked the girls a lot. After all, they were her friends, and they had even asked her to go to the mall with them. "If I do what you say, you'll be my friends?"

"Right," the girls said. "But you'd better do it right now, or we won't!"

They shoved the bag into Lisa's hand and gave her a nudge toward the jewelry counter.

Lisa looked back.

"Go on," the girls mouthed, smiling.

Lisa was at the counter, looking around. The salesgirl had her back turned. She was busy helping someone else. Jittery fingers reached out and slid a bracelet from the counter. It slipped onto the floor. Lisa became more scared. She looked at the girls. They were in another part of the store with their backs turned. Quickly Lisa picked up the bracelet, threw it in the bag, and went to meet her friends.

"Did you do it?" they asked. Lisa smiled weakly.

"Let's see." She opened the bag. The bracelet lay on top. "Cool! That wasn't so hard, was it?" Lisa wasn't so sure.

"The more you do it, the more fun it is," laughed one girl. "Right?"

The other girl giggled in agreement as they left the store.

In a matter of moments, the mall police came up and escorted the girls into an office. Lisa was horrified. Now the other girls looked scared, too. The police dumped both bags onto a large table. Out came sweaters, jewelry, cosmetics, and a handbag. The police asked many questions, and then called the parents.

Lisa's mother arrived first, and by this time, Lisa was sobbing with regret and fear. The other girls were silent. The police were serious. Stunned at hearing the tale, Lisa's mother asked the mall police what would happen to her daughter. Because of Lisa's age, and because it was a first offense, they said she could take her daughter home. Both Lisa and her mother assured the police it would never happen again. The other girls were asked to remain until their parents came and a decision concerning them could be made.

At first dumbfounded, Lisa's mother comforted her daughter, assured her of her love and forgiveness, and then began to talk gently to her about the meaning of true friendship. Lisa learned a lesson that day that she has not forgotten. In the years that have followed, with careful guidance from her mother, she has chosen friends more wisely, and she has never been involved in a similar incident.

Lisa was fortunate to have a mother who understood the strength of the peer pressure and who behaved with controlled reason. Some parents in this situation would have flown off the handle, screaming, "How could you do this to your father and to me?" This would only have humiliated the daughter further, causing her to withdraw into quiet anger at a time when she desperately needed loving support and guidance. Seeds of rebellion could have been planted in Lisa that would have thrown her into alliances with other "friends" and led her further astray through the years.

Schedule Pressure

Children today have a plethora of extracurricular choices. There are a host of sports to participate in all through the year with teams, leagues, a multitude of games, play-offs, and maybe even national tournaments. There are music and art opportunities galore and classes available for almost everything, for a fee. The dilemma comes in when families forget that *no child can be involved in everything.*

Some children are so involved in extracurricular activities, they hardly have time to attend school, much less to do the required homework. Such children become weary, anxious, and "burned-out" before they even turn twelve! And their stress carries over to siblings and parents as well.

Here again families have choices and consequences. Parents and children must decide together how many activities will be manageable for the family. Children need to decide which activities are the most appealing and prioritize their lists. Then the family needs to find out about the cost. Both the financial cost of participation and the expenditure of time need to be calculated in order to make wise decisions about family involvement. The family must find out what the schedules are for games, recitals, tournaments, shows, etc. Then, if the choices have conflicts, a plan must be chosen in advance to resolve those conflicts. Children also need to know in advance what the expectations are for kids in that program (e.g., practices, rehearsals, etc.) and the consequences when those expectations are not met.

Perhaps this kind of planning seems overly careful.

But consider the situation when a baseball player plays in two leagues and their games conflict. We've heard of an elementary-aged ball player actually leaving one play-off in the middle of the game to go to another game in another league's play-offs. Needless to say, the coach, the other parents, and the teammates were furious! With advance planning and good choices, such unfortunate consequences can be avoided.

Learning Teamwork, Doing Chores

Elementary children are at a great age to learn much about teamwork and the responsibilities it carries. For some, this is more of a struggle than others, but all of us need to incorporate this concept into our character in order to become fully mature.

Of course, kids hear coaches stress the importance of being a responsible team member in games and activities. What they may not realize is that the family is a team in the highest meaning of the word: A family must work together with coordinated effort, furthering the success of the family, with each member of the family choosing to subordinate personal prominence for the well-being of the entire family.

How can parents apply the teamwork concept at home? They must set up a system in which routine duties and chores are accomplished around the home for the good of the family as a team. Each person in the family is a team member who is responsible for various duties and chores. These differing responsibilities are determined by the age and capability of the individual family member. They need to know what Mom or Dad does at work and how the parents' jobs benefit the family team. They need to be made aware that the money earned pays for every part of their lives. Children need to know all that parents do inside the home and how this benefits the entire team. What would happen if Mom or Dad didn't cook, go to the grocery store, pay the bills, or repair the car? Letting the children know what's going on gives them a peek into the world of adult responsibilities and helps them to understand how their work in the family fits into the team concept. What kinds of chores can children do? They can make beds, pick up toys, clean sinks, and dump wastepaper baskets. A child of ten is able to make lunches. If the child fails to make the lunches, then that child will need to experience an appropriate consequence. Paying for the lunches that had to be purchased would be a logical consequence. The child could use allowance money for this or could earn money doing extra household chores to make up the deficit. Likewise, if other chores are neglected, logical and natural consequences can occur. If the trash is not put out, the child will find all the wastebaskets overflowing, and then it will be even more difficult to dump them. If toys are not picked up, they may "disappear" into Mom's closet for a week. If sinks are not cleaned, perhaps Dad will have to do it and charge the child a fee for each one done.

In Pat's family, the children were responsible for cleaning their own rooms. By the age of eleven, her son still needed to be reminded to clean his room while his eight-year-old sister had learned to clean well. Since her son was beginning to earn money outside of the home, Pat came up with an idea and discussed it with her daughter. Her daughter liked it, so Pat shared it with her son. "You have had years of training to clean your room. I still need to remind you. You are too old to be reminded. Therefore, you can either immediately begin cleaning your room each week, or you may pay your sister to clean your room. It's your choice."

Pat's son chose to pay his sister to clean, and that bargain continued through the remainder of the growing up years. (One note of hope for parents whose children are "slobs." Pat's son, who is now in graduate school, is able to clean fairly well. He still doesn't ever joyfully choose the activity, but he will do it now with a good attitude.)

It often helps a family team to have an ongoing discussion. Perhaps there are some changes, some exchanges of duties and responsibilities that can be made to increase the peaceful, smooth management of the team.

Choices about Religious Activities

A cause of concern for some conscientious, churchgoing parents is the dilemma when their children do not want to attend church or classes. The children make comments such as: "It's boring!" "It's too early!" "It lasts too long!" "My teacher's no good!" "I never have any fun when I go!" "I don't like the kids!" "The kids don't like me!" "Nobody talks to me!" "Do we HAVE to go?" "I'm too tired!" "Can't we stay home just this once?" "Can't we go [wherever] today?"

This situation is familiar in single-parent, as well as two-parent, homes. It is particularly difficult when one parent attends church with the children and the other does not. If the parent who does not attend encourages the children to go, it is most helpful. If the parent makes fun of the church experience and reluctantly tolerates the church attendance, the struggle for the children to attend becomes worse.

First, if at all possible, parents must choose together to commit themselves to attending services. Church attendance is a habit. Like any other habit it becomes stronger with use. In an environment of commitment, the children grow up without having a choice each weekend to attend or not to attend. Church attendance is like brushing teeth or going to school. As it is an integral part of family life, there is no alternative option to think about or to discuss.

Second, the choice for the child (and possibly the parent) is to have a good attitude about going, even if it's boring, too long, too early, and too full of mediocre teachers and kids who aren't nice. It is truly amazing how many aspects of life are long and boring and must be shared with some people who aren't interesting and with others who are hurtful. Chuck Swindoll asserts, "Life is ten percent what happens to me and ninety percent how I react to it. And so it is with you. . . . YOU ARE IN CHARGE OF YOUR ATTITUDES!"

Children can learn early in life that they are responsible for their attitudes and that they have a choice to be positive or negative. This applies not only to church attendance, but to every other "have-to" of life as well.

A third choice available to the family is to explore other churches to find one with different programs for children. If the children's programs are really poor, or inappropriate for your child, then that will be revealed in a frank discussion with the children. Don't cut a child off because you don't want to hear anything negative about church. Listen and find out what the true issues are. There may be some easy answers that crop up when you really talk about this. For example, children who are bored in the church service may find it helpful to have a quiet activity to do with their hands. Making friendship bracelets or doing mazes can make the time pass more quickly. And some children listen better when they have something to do!

Finally, in the church attendance dilemma can be found a great opportunity for children to take the mature step of choosing to find out what God wants them to learn. Many people need to learn that going to church does not mean waiting to be entertained. The interest generated by the average volunteer Sunday school teacher will never compare to an animated feature film. But the child can still benefit from learning about their family's faith and becoming friends with others in the church.

Perhaps the child who is having trouble needs to make a commitment to support the "boring, no-good" teacher in prayer during the week. If the child diligently follows through, praying for a better attitude as well as praying for the teacher and for the class, there will likely be a noticeable difference not only in the attitude of the child who prays, but also in the teacher and in the rest of the class.

7
Giving Choices to Teens and Young Adults

I came again when years were gone.
A man now I looked upon.
And he that early impress wore,
And I could change him never more.

Anonymous

The years of sowing seeds of good character in children come to a close between the ages of twelve and twenty. It's at this point that parents say, "How very quickly the years passed!" Time didn't seem to pass quickly during the infant and toddler years, when the sowing needed to be moment by moment, with very few breaks. The elementary years went by more rapidly, with school, church, and extracurricular concerns. But all that has passed away, and during the adolescent years, the parental harvest really begins. In fact, the reaping goes on for decades.

The adolescent/young adult years are times of extremely important choices, choices which will have a serious impact on the rest of the child's life and, like it or not, on the lives of the parents also. These choices include:

• Whether to take drugs, smoke, or drink

- When to date, whom to date, and what to do or not do on a date
- Whom to select for friends
- How to manage money
- If and where to go to college, what course of study to take, and what line of work to pursue

If parents have given the child the opportunity to benefit from choices and consequences all through the years, the adolescent will have the background necessary to make wise decisions. Now comes the time when talking "at" the child diminishes and listening increases as the young person verbalizes his or her inevitable personal, social, emotional, academic, and spiritual struggles. Just how much an adolescent will honestly share with the parent largely depends upon the foundation of love, trust, and honesty the parent has laid throughout the child's early life. This period of life, then, becomes a prime time for giving sparing but wise parental counsel concerning the monumental decisions that an adolescent will make.

Because of their struggle toward independence, teens are often accused of rebelling. A recent survey of high schoolers revealed they still consider their parents of great importance in their lives. What teens need, however, is guidance and honest, fair feedback, not lectures and the sort of imposed consequences they received earlier in life. (They do need to face the natural consequences of their actions, however.)

Listening, watching, and counseling a beloved child from the sidelines can be a tough role for a parent who has been actively involved in every aspect of the child's life. In fact, letting go is painful for both the parent and the child, but it is a necessary step in the maturation process.

The parent's most active and important role now can be as someone who prays for the adolescent. In the teen years, prayer is where the action is for parents. Never, ever give up. God's plans always take a lot longer than parents foresee!

Needs of Adolescents and Young Adults

Adolescence is well known as a time of great change and upheaval. In just a few years, teenagers must move from financial, emotional, and physical dependence to almost complete independence. All these achievements relate to the needs of the adolescent:

- Opportunities to explore and try out behaviors and areas of knowledge
- Adequacy in social relationships
- Competence in relationships with the opposite sex
- Increasing emotional distance from family
- Improving ability to make independent decisions
- Sense of direction in life
- Parents who support and encourage independence

Having an adolescent achieve independence is the assignment that creates so much conflict and confusion in families at this stage. But parents who have taught the child how to choose wisely in the small decisions and have allowed them to face the consequences of their choices through the years, will have prepared the adolescent/young adult for the major decisions of life he or she now must make.

Sean's Shirking

In this example of the common problem of procrastination, we see an opportunity that was misused, causing more damage than growth.

Sean's father was disgusted. Twelve-year-old Sean was the prince of procrastination. Sean always waited until the last moment to do everything, and this usually meant racing through chores or slopping through homework on the ride to school. Motivated by months of frustrating failures, Sean's father announced to his son one morning, "You are not—I repeat not—leaving this house today until your room is cleaned!"

The son was aghast. "What about the car pool?" he exclaimed.

His father countered, "They will just have to wait or leave you behind, so you'd better get working!"

Steaming and sputtering, Sean frantically began the work, accompanied by his father's tirade that he'd told him a thousand times . . .

When the car pool arrived, of course, Sean wasn't ready. The driver and two other boys waited a few minutes; then one boy came to the door to find out what was happening. Sean's father recounted the story, satisfied that he had arrived at a solution that would solve his son's problem of procrastination. But not everything went as planned. The car pool waited until a fuming Sean stormed out of the house yelling, "I hate my father! It's his fault if we're late to school! He never told me until this morning I had to clean my room before I left!"

The car pool finally did arrive at school. But three boys were late to class, and the driver was late to work.

There were several choices made in this situation. Sean made a wrong choice to procrastinate, postponing something he considered unpleasant so long that it eventually resulted in more pain for him and others. Because Sean's dad was frustrated with the situation, he gave Sean an ultimatum rather than a choice. The result was that rather than learning to establish an efficient work and play schedule, his son was humiliated and angered. Innocent car pool participants were also affected. They chose to wait, and all were late.

Sean's dad had other options for dealing with his son's problem. He could have given Sean a choice much earlier. He also could have driven Sean to school after Sean had finished his task, so that only Sean would be late to school. The father's ultimatum caused others to be late and was both inconsiderate and embarrassing, especially to Sean.

What we can see is that Sean's father waited much too long before giving a choice and consequence. He waited too many years. During those years, he should have been giving choices like this one: "You must get your room cleaned up. You can do it today before school, or you must come home after school and do it instead of getting together with your friends." Even when he did give a choice, this parent waited until he was ready to explode. It would have been so much better to deal with Sean's problem before it was an ingrained habit. Even so, Sean's dad could have made the situation one of growth for his son if he had handled it differently. An unemotional discussion with his son with plenty of advance warning and an appropriate time frame for the cleanup would have been responsible behavior that was also respectful of Sean and the members of the car pool.

Valerie Gets Dressed

In some families, differences of opinion about clothing and price can become either a battleground or an opportunity for adolescents to learn responsibility through choices and consequences. Fourteen-year-old Valerie loved clothes and was particularly attracted to certain designer labels. Any type of clothing—jeans, belts, bags, tops, undergarments—was that much better if the label was of a certain origin.

Valerie's parents did not object to their daughter being well dressed, but they were somewhat dismayed at the prices of the merchandise she preferred. Each year the prices escalated, along with Valerie's "needs." Something had to be done. Valerie's parents had a private talk about the problem and came up with what appeared to be a reasonable solution.

On a special "Dad 'n Daughter" evening, a time reserved for just the two of them that Valerie and her dad had establihed several years before, Valerie's dad presented the parents' idea. Valerie would be given a clothing allowance. They would give Valerie a certain amount of money in August so that she could purchase whatever she needed for the new school year. This money would be used to pay for all her wearing apparel, including such items as jewelry and shoes. Valerie's dad explained that they wanted her to have the freedom to spend the money in whatever way she desired and also to have the responsibility for using the money wisely.

Valerie loved the idea, so she and her dad discussed financial details. Her dad gave warnings about extravagance, emphasizing that she would not be given any money for clothing by either parent until the next installment in January. Valerie listened carefully, agreed to all stipulations, and the deal was done!

Then an ecstatic Valerie went shopping. At first the money seemed like a lot, but soon she realized that it wasn't enough for her tastes. She knew her parents meant what they said—there was no way she was getting any more money. So she had to make a list of priority items and select carefully. She had to decide whether it was more important to have another pair of expensive jeans or get the boots she wanted. The shopping expedition slowed down as Valerie was faced with more and more decisions of this type.

That afternoon she came home with fewer outfits than she had anticipated, but with a greater understanding of just how far money can go and why her parents wanted her to have control of the spending. She commented, "You guys were just hoping I'd find out about the value of money, weren't you?"

Her parents laughed and asked how the experiment was going. "Well, as you know," Valerie replied, "I absolutely *love* expensive stuff, but I figured out I will have to survive without some things I really thought I had to have. But I did get the really, really important things that I'll wear the most and that show the most. Do you get it?"

"Oh, we get it!" Valerie's parents gladly answered. They realized that this experiment was giving their daughter responsibility for the money as well as money management lessons that would benefit her for the rest of her life. They also noticed that Valerie's confidence grew as a result of the fiscal responsibility. And they continued this practice through adolescence with great success. (For another teenage money management story, please refer back to chapter 3.)

Nicholas's Grades

In some families, school grades are fertile ground for difficulties and therefore growth opportunities. Nicholas was not a good student, but he was capable of earning passing grades. What bothered his parents more than his poor grades, however, were the marks of U (Unsatisfactory) in cooperation. They firmly believed their son could get an S (Satisfactory) in cooperation and that a U was a reflection of an unacceptable attitude.

At the beginning of Nicholas's junior year, his parents told him that each U on his report card would cost him one hundred dollars worth of babysitting, payable at his usual babysitting rate per hour. There were two young children in his family, so there was always plenty of babysitting available for Nicholas. Nicholas agreed to try to improve, but he was positive that some of the teachers didn't like him, and he certainly didn't like them. His parents' advice? "Do your best and keep your mouth shut!"

When Nicholas turned sixteen, he enrolled in the driver's ed class. Within a short time, he became convinced that the teacher "did not like boys," and so, of course, she did not like Nicholas. Therefore, Nicholas didn't like her, and he made that feeling very obvious to the teacher.

His parents responded to this with disappointment and a warning: "Nicholas, whether the teacher likes you or not is immaterial. There will be many people along the way who may not like you, and you will need to learn to get along with them. Please do that now with this teacher. Keep yourself under control, don't say what comes to your mind, get an S, and save yourself a lot of unpaid work."

Not long after that, on a Sunday evening at nine

o'clock, Nicholas remembered that he was supposed to outline a chapter for the driving class. He moaned and groaned about it, asking his parents, "Do I have to do it?"

"Absolutely not," they replied. "It's your choice whether you ever do any work for the class or not. If you want to pass, you should do the work. If you don't care, and you want to repeat the class in summer school instead of going to basketball camp, then don't do the work."

Because it was late and he didn't feel like doing it, Nicholas chose not to outline the chapter (although he loved basketball camp and wanted to be on the team next year). Throughout the course there were various tests, and again and again, Nicholas made a choice. "I don't need to study this stuff. I already know enough."

Each time his parents responded, "It's up to you, Nicholas. You know the consequences of both an Unsatisfactory and a failure to pass the course."

What happened to Nicholas? Well, he got an *F* in his driver's ed course. In addition, he was given a *U* in cooperation, with a note from the teacher indicating that it was due to his sarcastic attitude.

Nicholas screamed, "Unfair! I don't deserve an *F.* I should get at least a *D.*"

His parents suggested, "If you feel it is unfair, then you need to make an appointment to see the instructor and discuss it with her."

At first, Nicholas determined to do just that. But after considering his test results and the several homework assignments he had chosen to ignore, he thought it best to leave things as they were. Nicholas could not go to basketball camp in the summer, and because of his *F* he was not eligible to try out for the team in the fall. He spent the summer babysitting and repeating driver's ed, with the same teacher!

It takes a courageous parent to watch a child make a poor choice that has serious future consequences and not scream or rescue the child from the responsibility of the consequences.

Diedre's Driving

For various reasons, parents sometimes make the fateful choice to protect their child from any and all consequences of their choices. This can result in some of the saddest stories imaginable. Here is one example.

When Diedre was nine, her mother died. Her distraught father was busy with his professional life, but he spent time with his daughter. He also provided a housekeeper, one who unfortunately was a poor role model and allowed Deidre to be in charge of the house and herself without much direction or guidance. Lacking the security of appropriate boundaries, Diedre grew into an extremely willful young woman.

Her father, feeling sorry for the motherless girl, developed a pattern of lecturing and rescuing. When Diedre was sixteen, he bought her a car, a brand new one. "Nothing is too good for my little girl!" her father emphasized.

It didn't take long for Deidre to receive too many traffic violations. Soon she was responsible for an accident that totalled the car. Because of his contacts with the police department, her father rescued her from the consequences. He lectured her severely, then bought her another new car.

Deidre's story doesn't end there. At seventeen, she developed a habit of selecting boyfriends who were objectionable to her father. "You just don't understand, Daddy!" was the response he received after one of his lectures. Nothing was resolved. Deidre continued to date the boys, and her father continued to lecture.

When Deidre was eighteen, she became pregnant. Her father was repulsed by the baby's father, who used drugs and was a heavy drinker. The boy was simply drifting through life with no goals. Deidre, however, was determined to marry him.

Shortly before the wedding, the boy was killed in a car accident caused by his drug and alcohol abuse. Deidre had the baby, but now she wanted a career. To make this possible for her, her father's new wife took care of Deidre's baby while Deidre went to college at her father's expense. Deidre was not expected to work for the tuition or to help pay any of her living expenses. Then, before completing the secretarial course, she dropped out, married, and immediately had another baby. At the age of twenty-five, Deidre tired of her husband and children, and she left them for another man.

Although her father disapproved strongly of her lifestyle and choices, he continued to finance both through the years, and he also continued to rescue her from the consequences of her actions.

We can only wonder what would have happened to Deidre if her father, rather than lecturing and rescuing, had allowed Deidre to assume the consequences of any of the disasters she created.

Glenn's Underachievement

As we've said earlier, standing back and letting our children choose and take responsibility for their choices can be some of the hardest work we will ever do as parents. The reward comes, however, when we watch children bridge the gap between adolescence and adulthood with a level of maturity that surprises everyone.

Glenn was brilliant, at least according to his achievement tests. But his grades were only average through high school, and this was a source of disappointment to his parents. Then, when he announced he was not planning to attend college, his parents were truly grieved.

"To think that someone with your potential for academic success would not attend college is tragic," they lamented. "You've not done well only because you have chosen not to apply yourself, but we know you can do the work."

"I know I can do the work too," Glenn replied. "But, for right now, I'm just not interested—mainly because I don't know what I want to do."

His parents were irritated. "Just how do you plan on

finding out what you want to do?" they inquired.

Glen took a deep breath and plunged ahead, "I've thought about this, and even though I know it will be hard for you to understand, please accept my decision. I plan to work for a steamship company and travel around the world until I see enough and know enough to make a decent decision about the rest of my life."

His parents were stunned. They couldn't believe what they were hearing. And they could barely imagine all the ramifications of what he said.

"Don't say anything right now," Glenn requested. "Think about it, talk about it, and try to see it from my viewpoint. I don't know what I want to do, and I do know I want to see the world. This is a way to do it."

Glenn's parents did think, pray, and talk about it. In fact, they spoke of little else for days, viewing the decision from every angle. They came to the conclusion that their son had done nothing wrong in choosing not to go to college and that perhaps Glenn's wanderlust would turn out to be just a postponement of his education. They gave their approval, and his high-school graduation celebration became a farewell party before his departure.

For over a year, Glenn traveled everywhere, communicating regularly with his family by letter, by telephone, and by the Internet. His parents appreciated being kept informed, and they felt content with the shipboard work he was doing. He was certainly seeing the world and learning much about people and places.

At long last, the call they'd been waiting for came. "I'm coming home," Glenn announced. "I've given notice to the steamship company, and I'll see you at the end of the month." His parents looked forward to the family reunion with great anticipation.

Glenn had been thinking about what to do with the rest of his life. During that time away, he had decided that the best way he could use his abilities and help needy people was to study anthropology and pursue a career in Third World development. "I have seen so much poverty around the world," he said. "I'd like to have a small part in relieving it. I hope I have your approval, because I'll need a lot of support in the years ahead."

Glenn's parents were elated. Their fondest dreams were going to come true, and all it took was time, patience, prayer, and understanding. Glenn's parents could have created enormous pressure on Glenn to attend college. Instead, they chose to respect his decision and encourage him, even though his plan did not coincide with theirs.

All too often, situations involving adolescents test the patience, endurance, and emotional stability of parents. Before reacting or overreacting, wise parents will remember to take these steps:

- Listen actively and objectively to the child.
- Keep quiet, striving for self-control and wisdom.
- Take time to assess the situation clearly and objectively.
- Continue to work for removal of anger and impulsivity, which will only result in scarred relationships.
- Consider all the options available. (Consulting with others who have come through similar situations with positive results is exceedingly helpful.)
- Review the consequences of what you will say before saying anything.
- Say what you mean and mean what you say.
- Be loving, fair, respectful, and consistent.
- Keep on looking for help from above.

8
How Giving Choices Keeps on Giving

Many of life's circumstances are created by three basic choices:
the disciplines you choose to keep,
the people you choose to be with,
and the laws you choose to obey.

Charles Millhuff

Jack was so excited! It was the day of his very first big race. He proudly put on his racing shoes and, with a big grin on his five-year-old face, joined the other children at the starting line. Sizing up the others in the race, Jack's mom and dad thought he had a pretty good chance of coming in at least second or third, maybe even first.

The command boomed over the loud speaker, "Get on your mark, get ready, get set . . . GO!" All the children dashed off at breakneck speed. Jack got off to a head start, running well, but then, something went wrong.

What was it? His mom and dad looked at each other with great concern. Jack was slowing down. Then he looked back at his parents with tears in his eyes. Could it be a sudden illness? Perhaps a piercing pain?

The other children were nearing the finish line as an embarrassed, tearful Jack hobbled to his parents. They comforted him, then gently asked, "What's wrong?" They wanted to know what could have happened to cause him to give up the race he'd anticipated for days.

"I-I didn't know where I was going," he stammered. His parents stifled a smile and assured him it was okay, that he had started off great, that next time he'd know exactly where the goal was ahead of time.

It's all too easy for parents to be like Jack. Moms and dads look forward to becoming parents, and they are thrilled when the child is born. The conscientious parents begin the awesome task of parenting, working diligently day by day, but do they know where they are going? Are they consciously working toward long-term goals of maturity for the children?

Giving children choices and consequences has an enormous advantage in helping parents to raise a child to be a responsible, mature adult. This approach helps parents:

- balance freedom and responsibility
- teach self-control
- guide the child
- encourage thinking before acting
- allow the child to ask questions and form opinions
- view happiness as a by-product of confidence
- provide consistency
- earn respect and trust

James Dobson says in *Hide or Seek*, "The parental purpose should be to grant increasing freedom and responsibility year by year, so that when the child gets beyond adult control, he will no longer need it."

Responsible parents desire to rear children who become mature adults. A friend, Pat McIntyre, shared a superb quote from Abigail Van Buren: "My Definition of Maturity: The ability to stick with a job without being supervised, the ability to carry money without spending it, and the ability to bear an injustice without wanting to get even!" Perhaps this quote could also be entitled, "The Dream of Every Parent with Grown Children."

Elizabeth George, an accomplished speaker and writer, has two daughters who were married within a year of each other. At the conclusion of each ceremony Liz and her husband were able to smile at each other, and say, "It is finished! Our work is done!"

How satisfying it must be for parents to know as their son or daughter marries or moves away that the parenting job has concluded and is complete. We all want to have our children reach adulthood without having to think, "Oh no! They aren't ready!" We want to achieve the goal of letting a young adult leave home believing that he or she is equipped to face the future. We believe that it is the parents who give choices and consequences through the years who will be able to let go of their adult children, confident that they have received essential preparation for facing life as adults.

A parent may legitimately ask, "If I consistently follow through with giving appropriate choices and consequences, can I be guaranteed that my child will emerge into young adulthood as a responsible person who will make good choices when I'm not involved?" The only honest answer is a resounding No!

Sometimes children will grow up and turn their backs on parental training. This can last for a mercifully short time, or it can be painfully long. Knowing that the child has been reared with choices and consequences can give the parents the hope and stamina to endure weariness, heartache, and discouragement. This knowledge can also help to alleviate the burden of parental guilt.

Ken and Alicia were young, enthusiastic parents who had all the answers. In their late twenties and thirties, as their three children were growing up, they taught parenting classes, led seminars at retreats, and even wrote a book. Why not? Why wait? They knew everything. After all, they were the perfect parents. And, naturally, their kids were perfect . . . until adolescence!

That's when their world of "perfect parenting of the perfect children" crashed! Over the next few years, each of their children succumbed to the temptations of youth, leaving their parents heartbroken.

During the following decade, Ken and Alicia were uncharacteristically silent. The simple answers to difficult questions did not fall so easily from their lips anymore. They were humbled and humiliated in their parenting. What had happened? Where had they gone wrong? They assumed, like so many people do, that parenting is like baking a cake. You put in the right ingredients, stick it in the oven, and it comes out the same way every time. Unfortunately, the results of the human condition are so complex that understanding the turmoil that really goes on in the heart of a growing child is more difficult than most of us ever realize.

Ken and Alicia were devastated by their experience. Their lives were shattered. Nevertheless, they determined to allow each of their children to fully experience the consequences of their unfortunates choices. They did not attempt to rescue them, but quietly endured their pain for their children and their bitter disappointment. People talked, analyzed, accused, and judged. Ken and Alicia waited and prayed.

During frequent bouts of despair, they wrestled with the parental demons of guilt. The *what ifs*, the *maybe we should haves*, the *if onlys*, the *where did we go wrongs*, the *when did it begins*, and the *why didn't we see the signs* haunted their days, invaded their sleep, and threatened to destroy their sanity.

After long months of futile introspection, Ken and Alicia swallowed their pride and went to a counselor with their heavy burden. They were weighed down not only with their own presumed guilt for imperfect child rearing, but also with guilt over the parental advice to others that had flowed so freely from their lips. The counselor was mature in years and in wisdom. There was very little he had not heard or seen before. He listened attentively to their outpouring and was able to give them comfort and insight. The counselor reminded them that :

• There is no perfect human parent. Even the most conscientious and determined parent will make mistakes.

- There is no way to totally control a child's environment. Even a car ride can result in an onslaught of negative stimuli which profoundly affects a protected child.

- There is no way to really know what is going on in the heart of a child. The most intuitive parent will, on occasion, misunderstand and misinterpret words and actions.

- Children possess free will. A child's decisions are not the simple result of good or bad parenting. The child makes free choices.

The counselor reminded Ken and Alicia that God is the only perfect Parent. God was perfectly consistent with Adam and Eve. He gave them choices and consequences. Yet his children made a profoundly poor choice. God wasn't surprised and did not love them less. But God did permit them to endure the consequences.

During the initial session with the counselor, Ken and Alicia shed many tears. And during the months that followed, they waited. But now they waited with a difference. They had hope.

In the years that have intervened, each of Ken and Alicia's children has come back, repentant, worn, and wiser. Although these grown children can never escape the consequences of their poor choices during their prodigal years, they have the forgiveness of God, their parents, and others. They are now leading productive lives. Whenever there is the slightest opportunity, they encourage teens to listen to their parents and to respect their decisions. They warn gullible teens of the tragic, lifelong consequences of rebellious choices.

What If You've Failed?

There are many parents who have not understood the concept of choices and consequences previously. They have erred in being either too permissive and placating, or excessively rigid and harsh. Their children may have gotten into serious problems as a result of those mistakes. As did Ken and Alicia, you may feel guilt over past parenting decisions and castigate yourself endlessly.

Is it too late for you? Never! As Grace's children grew up, she had to face the mistakes she had made. What she found to be most useful to them and herself was to seek forgiveness from them:

> By God's grace I discovered a few errors at a time. I was too demanding in some things; unwittingly I was too easy in others; I had even been known to rescue a child now and then! With each revelation I found time for a private talk with the child I had so inadvertently wounded. I apologized without trying to excuse myself, and I explained my motives. I owned the fact that my methods had sadly defeated my motives. I simply asked them to forgive me. They did.
>
> As my children became adults, I somewhat ceremoniously made the transition from Mom to friend. Granted, the changeover was marked with blunders, but my children will tell anyone that now we are friends indeed. We now exchange counsel and support of each other. We share both joy and sorrow, success and failure. I even hold hope that when I need to be "mothered" by them, they will be there for me.

It takes profound honesty, great courage, and utter transparency to complete the process of forgiveness. But both you and your children will be wiser and stronger for it.

No parents should ever be puffed up with pride because their child has not rebelled. Quite the opposite. Someone once asked the eminent pastor and author Charles Stanley, "When will I know if I've been a good parent?" The answer is priceless, and it's one that should keep all parents humble: "You will know if you've been a good parent when your grandchildren's children become parents!"

There is one thing we know right now, however. The sooner parents begin to use the gift of choice with their child, the sooner they will see positive results. Parents have a wonderful opportunity to positively affect both present and future generations. There isn't a better time to start than right now!

Appendix

Choices and Consequences: God's Parenting Tool

Searching through the Bible, we find out something amazing about the gift of choice and consequence. This principle is everywhere from Genesis through Revelation. We can even see it as God's Principle of Parenting. It all began with Adam and Eve. God gave them great authority and freedom, and only one little rule. God told them there was only one fruit of one tree they needed to avoid. Everything else was permitted. Adam and Eve had a choice to obey or to disobey. God gave them the power of choice, and he also told them the consequence well in advance! They could never claim that God was unfair or that they didn't know.

Later, in Deuteronomy 11:26-28, God confirms that gift of choice in words to his people,

> See, I am setting before you today a blessing and a curse—the blessing if you obey the commands of the Lord your God that I am giving you today; the curse if you disobey the commands of the Lord your God and turn from the way that I command you today by following other gods, which you have not known. (NIV)

It is very obvious that God wants his children to obey him. Yet God the Father does not *make them obey*. He gives his children the choice. To encourage them to obey, he promises blessings, the positive consequences of obedience. These very specific blessings are listed in the first fourteen verses of Deuteronomy 28, and they are things that his children really want!

God also lists specific negative consequences which will follow if his children make the poor choice to disobey. These unfortunate consequences are listed in Deuteronomy 28:15-68. If you read this sobering list, you will undoubtedly shudder.

This principle of giving choices and consequences makes sense in a parent-child relationship, but there is something truly astonishing about God's treating human beings this way. The almighty, supreme power of the universe, the One who can do anything, anywhere, at any time, does not *make* his human creation obey, but gives power of choice. Why would he do that?

The explanation must be that God, the merciful Parent and magnificent Creator, has such love and respect for human beings, persons created in his image, that he wants them to obey out of hearts of love and gratitude for who he is and what he has done. Had God withheld the gift or the power to choose, humankind would have consisted of beautiful, intelligent robots—mechanical people, incapable of feeling, striving, and conquering.

Because of his great love, God is eager to honor obedience with positive consequences, but he also allows his children to experience the consequences of their poor choices. Why? A well-chosen consequence stimulates obedience. Psalm 119:67 exemplifies this concept, "Before I was afflicted I went astray, but now I obey your word" (NIV). The psalm writer declares what we all know, and regretfully admit, about ourselves and our children—without appropriate consequences for our behavior, human beings choose the road of ease and rebellion. The discipline of God the Father encourages us to take a different road, the road of obedience. Robert Frost in one of his most famous poems described the "road less traveled." Taking that less-traveled road will make a great difference to our lives.

As a parent, God trains his children for future work. He always has the big picture in mind. Likewise, as parents, our goal cannot be to do what gets us through the day. We must always look down the road. Our children's future, whether good or evil, may be largely determined by the choices and consequences we construct for them.